T0383461

Universal Principles of UX

100 Timeless Strategies to Create Positive Interactions between People and Technology

Irene Pereyra

Consider

Empathize

Define

Research

Design

Validate

Most jobs have an easy-to-understand title you can quickly mention and move on from with no risk of confusion, and most job titles don't require lengthy explanations. I'm a photographer. I'm a teacher. I'm a zoologist. People nod, say something polite like "That must be interesting!", take a sip of their drink and continue the conversation. "I am a UX designer," however, almost always results in raised eyebrows followed by a rambling monologue where I try to explain the complexity, expansiveness, and evolving nature of the field.

"You know what an architect does? UX designers—or user experience designers—are basically architects, but instead of designing physical structures, we design digital structures. And just as architects don't actually physically build the buildings they design, we also rely on programmers and developers to build the digital structures we design."

However incomplete my architect analogy may be, user experience design is not a new concept. Some claim the term was first coined by Don Norman in 1993 for his new job as User Experience Architect at Apple, whereas others say it was first described in a 1987 usability engineering journal by John Whiteside and Dennis Wixon.

The exact origin of the term may be debatable, but the fact that the practice of user experience design goes back a long time is not.

When the Greek physician Hippocrates wrote how a surgeon's tools should be arranged for optimal use in operations, or mechanical engineer Frederick Winslow Taylor analyzed workflows in order to increase productivity while reducing work related injuries, or media mogul Walt Disney and his team of "Imagineers" put themselves in their guest's shoes so they could create magical and immersive park experiences, they were all acting as user experience designers.

Perhaps the best predigital-era example of someone thinking of the user experience comes from 1955. Industrial designer Henry Dreyfuss famously wrote, "When the point of contact between the product and the people becomes a point of friction, then the designer has failed. On the other hand, if people are made safer, more comfortable, more eager to purchase, more efficient—or just plain happier—by contact with the product, then the designer has succeeded."

Now if you imagine that the product he mentioned could also be a digital product like email or online dating, or buying airline tickets, or shopping for a new pair of shoes, and you replace the word *people* with *users*, you basically have the framework for user experience design today.

But here's the catch. Ask ten different people to define user experience design today, and you'll receive ten different answers. Unlike architecture, which has had thousands of years to mature and to be defined, we are still in the infancy of defining what this field actually is. Not to mention that experiences are inherently subjective, and that we design digital services, products or tools—not experiences—that we hope will *result* in the intended experience.

To make matters worse, during my many years of teaching user experience design, I realized a lot of the books and articles that cover this topic tend to be written from the outside-in, with the author compiling a list of examples that describe a process they were not actually a part of—a theoretical utopia. It's also almost always written in a way that makes it seem like there is a perfect way of doing things, and if you don't do it that way you're doing it wrong. But the perfect UX process does not exist. There is no one definition of UX design, the same job title can mean different things at different companies, and the answer to almost every question is "it depends."

This book is not a chronological retelling of the history of user experience design. It is also not a technical how-to book that will show you how to become a perfect user experience designer one step at a time. It's a philosophical anthology of case studies, situations, problems, and contradictions I've encountered across more than fifteen years of working on real-world client projects that will teach you how to think, rather than tell you what to do. And in the spirit of the internet, it's up to you whether you want to go through these sequentially, or jump around topics you find interesting.

But there is one thing we can all agree on: User experience is about users. So let's start there. Who are they anyway? And why should we care? Understanding the needs, goals, desires, and motivations of these real human beings—everyone who interacts with and is affected by these digital products—is the first step in getting closer to untangling the contradictory field that is user experience design.

We log more scr
we do sleeping,
or checking em
people to resist
and alcohol.

en time than
nd tweeting
s is harder for
an cigarettes

01

The user comes first.

When I first started working as a UX designer, I remember feeling a bit icky about the term "user." For most people it probably holds more negative connotations than positive ones. Drug users, people who use other people. By itself, the word *user* only implies that someone is using something. And for a field that claims to be the design advocate for real-life human beings, calling those human beings "users" sounds vague and dehumanizing.

Unfortunately there isn't a better alternative. "Individuals" and "people" are too broad and generic, "entities" feels like legalese and "actors" is too confusing. More specific labels like readers, enthusiasts, investors, or employees might make it easier to relate while designing, but until those exact needs and motivations have been defined, we still need a generic way to address people. "Users" is the best we've got.

Regardless of what we call the people who will use our products, the reason we need to keep the actual human beings—or users—front and center is to ensure the wrong decisions don't get pushed through because of the personal opinions of the business stakeholder or, worse, the assumptions of the designer. To keep everyone's irrelevant opinions and assumptions at bay, and put the attention back on the user, we start every project with the following questions:

Who is it for (the audience)?
Why will they use it (the goal)?
How will they use it (the context of use)?

Early on in my career, I worked on the web interface for one of Electronic Arts' (EA, the leading American video game company) college football games. I didn't know anything about American football—let alone college football—and I wasn't given any time to talk to potential users. I decided to do some guerilla research on my own and reached out to a couple of college friends who I knew were massive football fanatics. The insights I discovered after two weeks of asking questions ended up making the final experience far more effective than if I would have tried to design it based on my own assumptions alone.

Putting the user first does not require anything other than the dedication to do so. We don't need a whole lot of fancy processes to walk a mile in our user's shoes. We just need to listen more, and talk less. And ask smart questions (see Principle 57). And be curious. And be empathetic. Including the end-user into our process from the start will help us solve problems in a way that will have a real impact on the very real people who interact with our designs.

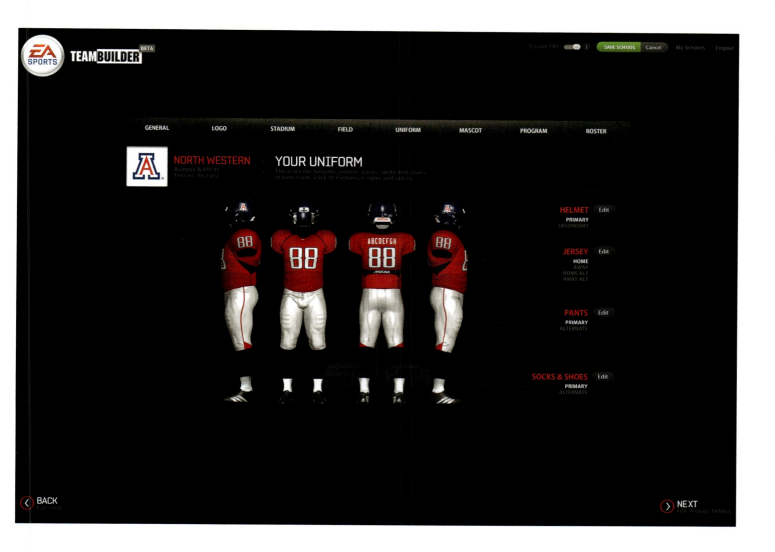

→
NCAA Football 11 was released in 2010 on all consoles, with the exception of the Wii, and it was the only version ever released for iOS. Teambuilder was a feature accessed through the EA Sports Teambuilder website, allowing users to customize logos, uniforms, fields, stadiums, mascots, programs and rosters. Teams that were made via the site could be downloaded by other users and could be played with on the console.

02

Work on UX and UI simultaneously.

The most contested topic within our industry is the "UX versus UI" debate. What's the difference? What is more important? Who should do what? Things were a lot easier in the early 2000s—before the mainstream adoption of these terms—when designing for the web simply meant you were a web designer. As the industry expanded and matured, terminology had to be adjusted to include the wider spectrum of devices, gestures, contexts, and screen sizes, and the role of the designer needed more definition.

The core argument is centered on whether one designer can—or should—do both, and how much of the foundational UX design needs to be completed before starting the visual UI design. In our studio this is not up for debate. One designer focuses on the UX, and another on the UI, while working simultaneously on both. Why?

Let's revisit the architect analogy. We first need to determine whom the building will be for, and what those people plan on doing. We also need to understand the landscape by looking at benchmarks and competitors. Then we need to create a blueprint that establishes how many floors there will be, where the doors and stairs are, how each room relates to the next, how to make it accessible for people with disabilities, and so on. In short, UX design is the foundation or blueprint that considers the user's needs, wants, behaviors, and contexts. This work requires a certain type of thinking and a certain type of designer. (Interestingly, the Zulu, the term for architect, *umqambi wesino*, means "magician of space," "maker of a situation," or "maker of a sensation").

But the foundation alone will not make the building fully functional. We still need to choose the color of the walls, select a floor that looks attractive and is easy to clean, pick furniture that makes the place feel unique, hang picture frames in a visually pleasing manner and remove obstacles so it's accessible for people using wheelchairs. Making something usable and digestible through visual design is the user interface, and that kind of work requires a different kind of thinking and a different kind of designer.

If we don't work on these two components of the design simultaneously, we can't play to the strengths of each discipline, and we can end up with a final building that feels either uncomfortable or illogical. The reason UX and UI need to collaborate closely on the entire experience from beginning to end is to ensure all efforts are always moving in the same direction. Since UI owns the final presentation of the product, and that final presentation has an impact on the overall user experience, why would we even want to separate them? Don't we want a final design that's usable *and* attractive? (See Principle 8.)

→
The "Building" page is shown from the M+ museum in Hong Kong, which tells the story of the design of the building by Swiss architects Herzog & de Meuron. The wireframes (left) were done by the user experience designer, whereas the final UI (right) was done by the UI designer. However, we ask for approval by the client on the wireframe level so that we don't yet have to worry about final copy and images since that takes much longer to finalize.

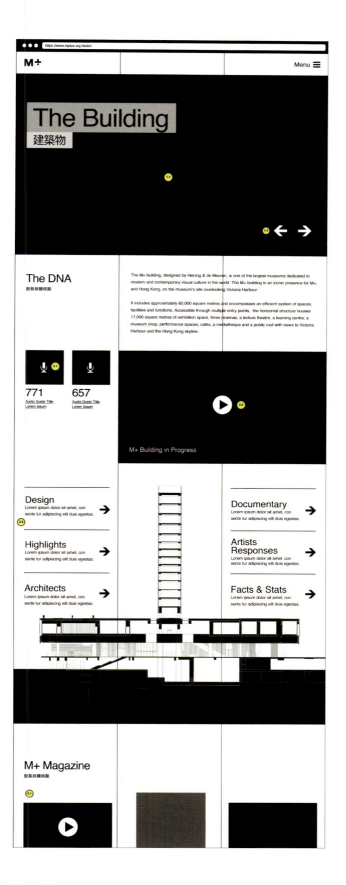

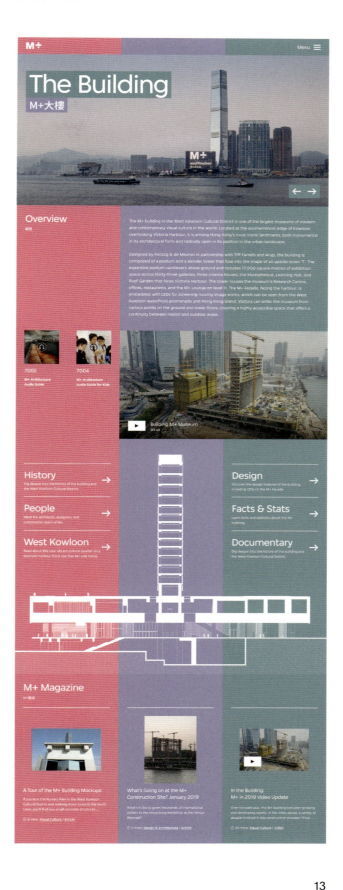

03

UI makes or breaks usability.

Any product any designer creates is first and foremost measured by the effectiveness of its usability. Or in other words, how well a user can use that particular design helps them achieve their intended goal. Why? Because products, services, and messages that don't work are annoying at best and disastrous at worst.

Since UX is about the totality of the experience a user has with a product or service, we tend to think high usability is achieved by simply focusing on UX. However, it's a different discipline—UI—that is responsible for what end-users will actually interact with. Choices in things like layout, typography, information hierarchy, interactions, accessibility and information density is the responsibility of the UI designer, and that's what ultimately makes or breaks usability (see Principle 75).

Remember the 2000 presidential election in the United States where Bush won by a small 537-vote Floridian margin? Turns out the misaligned rows in the now infamous "butterfly" ballot caused many people to accidentally vote for the wrong candidate. Bad usability in both UX *and* UI caused Al Gore to lose the presidency.

Let's evaluate where each discipline dropped the ball:

- Difficulty in registering to vote: UX fail
- Poorly designed polling places: UX fail
- Lack of consistency in voting mechanics from year to year: UX fail
- Lack of accessibility for hearing and visually impaired: UX and UI fail
- Low learnability for first-time voters: UX fail
- Low learnability for people with low digital literacy: UX fail
- Confusing instructions: UX fail
- Biased order of candidates (first items in a list are favored): UI fail
- High cognitive load (too many options presented at once): UX and UI fail
- Confusing ballot layout design: UX and UI fail
- Lack of visual hierarchy: UX and UI fail
- Poor legibility with chosen typography: UI fail
- Malfunction of punch-card mechanism leaving hanging chads: UX fail

People often confuse usability with user experience and ease of use. But usability needs to be taken into account throughout the entire design process—from wireframes to the final interface—by both UX and UI designers. Maybe if somebody had done some usability testing on both the UX of the voting experience, as well as the UI of the actual ballot design, this entire mess could have been avoided, and Al Gore would have been president.

04

Always surpass expectations.

The first time I traveled through Singapore's Changi Airport, I thought to myself that whoever designed this would make an amazing user experience designer. The airport is a destination in itself, with waterfalls and gardens, open-air decks, and a variety of amazing restaurants. There's even a swimming pool. It was the first time in my life where I had a conscious feeling of "whoa, that's cool" at an airport. I was sad to board my plane.

The worst airport I've ever had the misfortune to travel through is LaGuardia Airport in New York City. The low ceilings, narrow corridors, drab and stained carpets, and lack of proper dining options make for such a terrible travel experience that I already start to feel depressed on the taxi ride there. However, at their core, LaGuardia Airport and Changi Airport offer the exact same functionality—they're both a hub for air travel. Yet one is infinitely better than the other.

Every year I give my students—who are doing a master's in interaction design—the exact same brief. I give them the same information, the same input, and the same restrictions. Every year they do a great job of focusing on usability, content, and functionality, but they don't think about that little extra that can make an interaction feel unique or memorable. All of their first design solutions are totally forgettable. Only when they learn to start looking at the problem from a different angle, are they able to make it special (see Principle 41).

Don't get me wrong. A product must first, before anything else, work. Otherwise it's just putting lipstick on a pig. But merely making a product work is just table stakes. That may have been enough back in the late 1990s and early 2000s when there were literally a handful of options to choose from, but in today's landscape, where there are close to ten million mobile apps alone, a usable product that is not memorable is just not going to cut it.

So what constitutes a positive and memorable experience? Two things: First, we need to come up with features people won't expect, like when Steve Jobs introduced the pinch-to-zoom functionality during a 2007 Apple event (the crowd literally gasped). Second, we also need to get people into a state of flow, which psychologist Mihály Csíkszentmihályi described as a state of complete immersion. According to Csíkszentmihályi, if people are completely involved and focused on what they are doing, activities become more engaging and enjoyable.

In other words, if we can manage to surprise users with intuitive and innovative features, and if the interaction model eliminates distractions and gets people into a state of flow, we are one step closer to surpassing their expectations.

→
For the tech-enabled talent management company True, we created a surprising interaction model. Each letter in the word *true* reacts to the user's mouse cursor, and as the user scrolls down the page, the background remains, moving only the white component up, while revealing the background image through the cut-out of the circle, triangle, and square.

placing & growing talent around the world

overview

team

our story

news

join

contact

True Search

We place executives and other strategic talent for the world's most innovative organizations.

find talent

Thrive

We've built powerful talent management technology for enterprises, investment firms, and recruiters.

gain insights

Synthesis

Helping leaders and teams reach their full potential, make better talent decisions, and increase value creation.

develop leaders

05

Design is
not neutral.

In the early days of the internet, Nigerian princes emailed to borrow money, sweepstakes pop-ups guaranteed our winnings, and crushes would be revealed if we opened ILOVEYOU.txt. Those scams were not very subtle, and were not unlike psychic infomercials on TV, radio ads announcing free holidays, fake money orders being sent in the mail, or Mandarin robocalls targeting Chinese immigrants in the United States.

Today the internet is much more subtle in tricking us into doing things we don't want to do. Unlike the old scams, it's usually not as blatant as asking for money. It's little deceptive tricks used by legitimate companies meant to generate more sales, get more subscribers, or gather more personal information. It's ordered by companies, carefully crafted with a solid understanding of human psychology, executed by designers, and perfectly legal.

Almost every country in the world has an ethics code for psychologists, doctors, lawyers, and the media. Some have it for engineering and real estate. But in design, there is no such thing. In 2010, UX designer Harry Brignull (PhD, cognitive science) coined the term "dark patterns" (I personally prefer the term "deceptive patterns") and listed twelve examples that are deliberately designed to deceive. Some are quite harmless, like a "subscribe to newsletter" checkbox that is selected by default, whereas others—like ads designed to appear as regular news articles—are potentially very dangerous.

When we started our studio, we made the deliberate decision to not work for clients that actively harm the environment (like big oil), human beings (like pharma), or society as a whole (like a certain large social media platform that contributes to the spread of fake news and conspiracy theories). But sometimes ethical considerations are less obvious, more of a slippery slope and more insidious.

When we were working with an internationally respected and well-known magazine—yes, you know who they are—we were asked to design "native advertising" templates. Native advertising is ads designed to look exactly like real articles, making it deliberately more difficult for people to differentiate between news and advertising. It felt wrong, we brought it up, and our concerns were dismissed. I'm ashamed to say that we didn't stand our ground, and that in the end, we went ahead with their request. This was many years before the whole fake news crisis, but I often look back on that moment and wonder if I contributed to the problem.

Since there is no ethics code in design, we have to rely on each individual designer to make the right moral decision. If our designs deliberately hide true costs, trick people into decisions, or misrepresent information, we are part of the problem. It doesn't matter if it's not our company or we're doing it for a client—we're responsible. It's easy not to take on new clients we don't agree with. It's much harder to stand our ground when an existing client asks us to design something we know is inherently wrong and harms society.

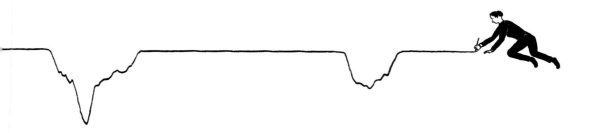

06

Words matter.

I always tell my students that the best skill to invest in as a UX designer is writing. The internet is made up of words afterall. Good UX copy is written to be felt and is the opposite of technical jargon. It's meant to evoke emotion, while simultaneously removing all ambiguity. It's an extremely important part of the user experience, and its absence is deeply felt. Without the right words, the entire user experience crumbles.

According to research done by eMarketer in 2020, we now log more screen time than we do sleeping. Most of us spend more time communicating with interfaces than we do with actual human beings. When that communication feels natural, we take it for granted. But when it feels even slightly weird or nonsensical, we're instantly turned off.

Unfortunately for all of us, bad UX copy is everywhere. We are constantly being bombarded with messages and demands for information that can range from the existential to the bizarre. Pop-ups from the operating system asking us where we are. Uber notifies us that Jesus is now arriving in a Honda Accord. Facebook tells us we have zero friends. What?

You may have heard the common misconception that people don't read on the web. That's incorrect. People do read on the web. They just read differently. They tend to be more task oriented and goal focused than when reading print (see Principle 75). They also expect more of a conversation, since unlike print, they have the ability to go back and forth with the system. So they want to get stuff done quickly, and communicate the way they would if a computer wasn't involved.

When writing for the web, the North Star should always be to make the copy as digestible and conversational as possible. Simplify language, label content, make copy bite sized, don't bury links in long paragraphs, and ensure content is easy to scan. Bonus points if you use lists. People love lists. And go ahead and address the user directly with "you." The word *you* makes it about them and their goals, and not about you and your product or service.

It's also very important to be ruthless about editing, both on the sentence level and the paragraph level. Cut it down so it says exactly what it needs to say, nothing more. Once you feel good about it, try reading it out loud. Good copy for the web should feel conversational. If it feels weird or robotic when you read it out loud, you're not quite there yet.

→
For the interactive survey we worked on in collaboration with SPACE10/IKEA that was meant to capture and display people's preferences around communal living (One Shared House 2030), we created an interface that allowed people to quickly filter through all the data through conversational language.

Universal Principles of UX

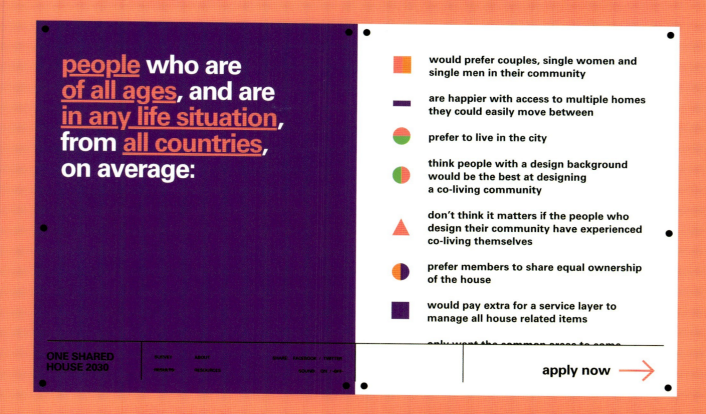

people who are **of all ages**, and are **in any life situation**, from **all countries**, on average:

- would prefer couples, single women and single men in their community
- are happier with access to multiple homes they could easily move between
- prefer to live in the city
- think people with a design background would be the best at designing a co-living community
- don't think it matters if the people who design their community have experienced co-living themselves
- prefer members to share equal ownership of the house
- would pay extra for a service layer to manage all house related items
- only want the common areas to come

ONE SHARED HOUSE 2030

SURVEY ABOUT
RESULTS RESOURCES
SHARE FACEBOOK / TWITTER
SOUND ON / OFF

apply now →

women who are **40—59**, and are **single parents**, from **...** on a**...**

hong kong
hungary
iceland
india
indonesia
iran

reset filters

- would prefer teenagers in their community
- are happier with access to multiple homes they could easily move between
- prefer to live in the city
- think people with a design background would be the best at designing a co-living community
- don't think it matters if the people who design their community have experienced co-living themselves
- prefer members to share equal ownership of the house
- wouldn't pay extra for a service layer to manage all house related items
- only want the common areas to come

ONE SHARED HOUSE 2030

SURVEY ABOUT
RESULTS RESOURCES
SHARE FACEBOOK / TWITTER
SOUND ON / OFF

apply now →

07

Visual metaphors communicate the fastest.

An image is processed 60,000 times faster than text, and is filtered through the lens of our mind—mental models, which are simplified versions of the world around us (see Principle 62). A good visual metaphor creates new meaning out of these mental models and helps audiences relate by tapping into existing symbolism.

Right after the massive 9.0 earthquake and subsequent tsunami hit Japan in 2011, we started working on a website for Google Japan that would allow people from all over the world to send messages of hope to the Japanese people while raising funds to help disaster efforts. On the "Messages for Japan" website, people were able to write notes in their own language that were translated in real time through the integration of the Google Translate API.

Google was also going to be running ads to raise awareness for the campaign, and considering the high amount of ad saturation—and the fact that Google Translate is not inherently visually interesting—there was extra pressure on us to choose the right visual metaphor to quickly cut through the noise.

So we asked ourselves, what immediately communicates "Japan" and "hope"?

After doing very quick research—the site had to be launched within 48 hours—we settled on the Japanese cherry blossom tree. Cherry blossoms symbolize spring, a time of renewal, and the fleeting nature of life. We quickly discussed it with the Google Japan team to make sure we were not inadvertently being culturally insensitive, and when we got the green light, we immediately got to work.

At its core, the purpose of the site was pretty straightforward. However, the messages were designed to look like the flowers of a cherry blossom tree, and the more messages were being left, the more the tree would start to bloom. We knew this campaign would have a very short and very intense amount of traffic, so it was amazing to see that for the first two weeks after the earthquake hit, the symbolic cherry blossom tree was in full bloom.

When the campaign ended, over 50,000 messages from over forty different countries had been translated, and over $5 million was raised in donations. It was the first time Google Translate was not used as a utility but rather as a way to express the better part of our humanity. The success of the campaign was largely—if not entirely—due to us choosing a visual metaphor that quickly conveyed the right message.

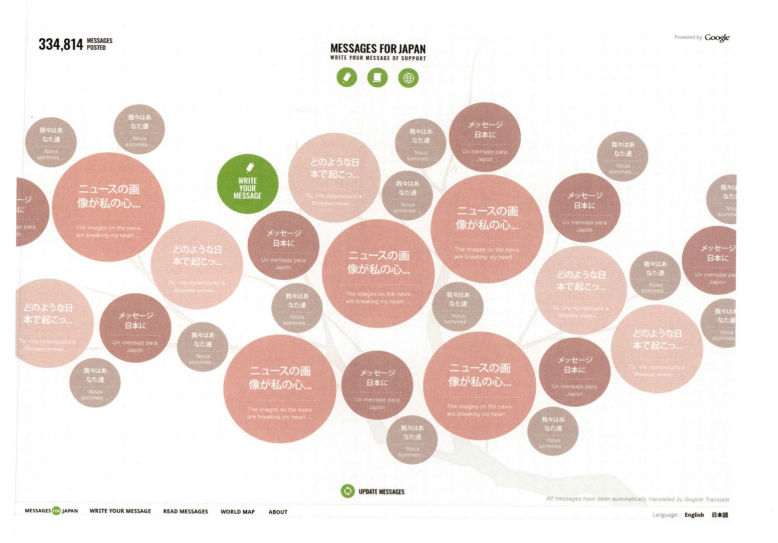

334,814 MESSAGES POSTED

Powered by Google

MESSAGES FOR JAPAN
WRITE YOUR MESSAGE OF SUPPORT

WRITE YOUR MESSAGE

UPDATE MESSAGES

All messages have been automatically translated by Gogole Translate

MESSAGES FOR JAPAN WRITE YOUR MESSAGE READ MESSAGES WORLD MAP ABOUT

Language: **English** 日本語

→
The interactive experience we worked on for Google Japan
allowed people to leave messages in their own language
for the people affected by the 2011 tsunami that devastated
Japan. The stylized Japanese cherry blossom tree was in
bloom with messages for people from all over the world
to read.

Consider

23

08

Attractive products are more usable.

Most of the scientific research on how human beings interact with computers has been done in the field of human-computer interaction (HCI), not by UX designers. These research studies are controlled, grounded in real science, and conducted without any particular bias or agenda.

In 1995 Japanese HCI research scientists Masaaki Kurosu and Kaori Kashimura tried to understand the correlation between usability and aesthetics in computer interactions. They asked 252 participants to judge twenty-six different ATM interfaces based on ease of use and how aesthetically pleasing the interface was perceived to be.

The results of the study indicated that people don't judge usability based on how usable the interface actually is. We judge usability based on aesthetics.

In other words, we are biased to believe that beautiful products work better, even if they don't. And when they don't, we still think they are beautiful and are far more forgiving of any potential usability issues we might encounter in the product later on. This phenomenon has been observed and confirmed in many more studies since, and is called the aesthetic-usability effect.

The most unusable product we have ever designed in our studio is also one of the most beautiful—the NU:RO watch. The watch has two dials, one with hours at the top, and the other with minutes at the bottom. Each dial has its own crown to adjust either the hour or the minute, but not both at the same time. And because minutes are only shown in intervals of five, it's almost impossible to tell time accurately. Yet no one has ever returned one complaining about its poor usability.

The NU:RO watch might not be very easy to use, but neither is a Leica camera, Philippe Starck's Juicy Salif lemon squeezer, or the aptly named Lamborghini Diablo. We don't mind putting in the effort, because we value their beauty more.

This doesn't mean we can focus on only making things beautiful and call it a day. Our willingness to forgive does have its limits. If something doesn't work at all, or if users can't find what they're looking for, no amount of beauty will save it (see Principle 13). If there is a real lesson to be learned here, it's not that we should focus on only making things beautiful while ignoring usability, it's to understand *why* we should focus on both.

→
A close-up of our self-produced NU:RO watch that tells the time in the middle of the hourglass. It's not the most intuitive design, but it's certainly a beautiful one.

09

People remember the unusual.

French-American industrial designer Raymond Loewy claimed people are torn between a fear of anything too new and a curiosity about new things. He called this the MAYA principle (an abbreviation for Most Advanced Yet Acceptable) and stated that to sell something new, you need to make it familiar, and to sell something familiar, you need to make it surprising.

If, for example, we're introducing a brand-new product to market, like vegan eggs that are made from mung beans, we probably want to design packaging that is as close to regular chicken eggs as possible. But if we're selling regular chicken eggs next to a bunch of other regular chicken eggs, we want our packaging to stand out and be different.

In 1933 German psychiatrist Hedwig von Restorff conducted memory experiments and discovered that when people were given a list of words to remember, they were more likely to remember the word that stood out. Whether it was longer than the rest, in a different typeface, in italic, or in a different color didn't matter. It just had to be different. In fact, the weirder it was, the more it was remembered.

This bias is called the Von Restorff effect and is what we used to distinguish ourselves from our competitors when we started our own design studio, Anton & Irene. We knew we were going to have to compete for clients against thousands of larger, more established, and better known digital agencies, while still basically offering the same services. In other words, we were selling eggs next to a bunch of other eggs, except that nobody had ever heard of our eggs.

We looked at the portfolio websites of our competitors and realized they were all using similar type treatments, layouts, storytelling methods, and even headshots. It was a bland sea of more of the same. Standing out from this particular crowd was not going to be that difficult.

We put on colorful skintight bodysuits and created a sequence of images that would react, depending on where the user would hover. Instead of headshots, we photographed ourselves in fencing outfits in the snow. It was a homepage unlike any other, and it worked. Whenever we ask our clients why they chose us in particular, they almost always answer "your website was just so . . . *different."*

Every time we make an item visually stand out, deliberately draw attention to something, or highlight important information in a group, we are using this bias (see Principle 15). And since most of the time we're not working on brand-new or unprecedented products, the easiest way to make an impact is by simply doing the opposite of whatever everyone else is doing.

→
The homepage and bio images of our studio's website (Anton & Irene), with my design partner, Anton, on the left, and me on the right, are unlike any other agency's imagery. Both images can be interacted with through the user's mouse cursor and were shot in camera.

Universal Principles of UX

10

First and last items are remembered most.

In 1885 German psychologist Hermann Ebbinghaus conducted memory experiments on himself to examine whether the position of an item in a list affected his ability to recall it. He discovered that it's easier to remember items that are either at the beginning or at the end of a sequence. That's because items that are at the beginning of a sequence are stored in our long-term memory, and items that are at the end of a sequence are stored in our short-term memory. Our brain doesn't quite know what to do with the stuff that's in the middle.

This bias is called the serial position effect and is vital when designing any kind of information online. If we need users to remember something in particular, or if there is a specific action we need them to perform, it's probably a good idea to either lead or end with that and not bury it somewhere in the middle.

During the global COVID-19 pandemic, we were asked by Adobe to mentor an aspiring young creative on a project. The project we settled on would allow users to navigate news articles and social media posts that mention how people's perception of time had changed during the pandemic. Starting with March 2020, users were able to navigate through the remaining pandemic months, culminating in a survey that asked people whether their perception of time had changed.

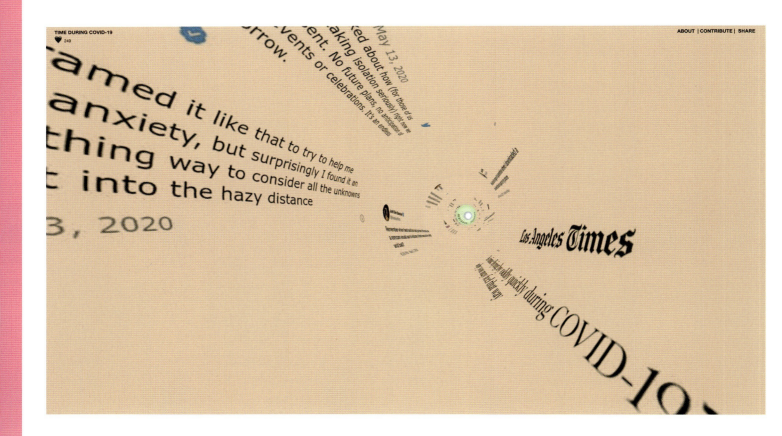

To quickly communicate what this project was about, we put the description of the project first. The news articles were organized chronologically through the *z*-axis of the screen—like a tunnel—to entice users to skip through and get to the end as quickly as possible. Once they reached the end of the tunnel, they were prompted to complete the survey. The most important thing we wanted them to *remember* came first, but the most important thing we wanted them to *do* came last.

Understanding how memory works—and using the serial position effect to our advantage—is vital in UX. Not everything can be equally important. Besides ensuring that all information is scannable and bite size (see Principle 6), we need to decide what it is we want people to remember or do and put that either first or last in a sequence. Any interaction model we design needs to deliberately allow users to forget the not-so-important parts to make space for what we want them to remember.

↓
The "Time During Covid-19" interaction model is meant to generate a sense of claustrophobia that makes people want to get to the end as quickly as possible, similar to how most of us felt during the global pandemic. Since we wanted people to tell us how they felt during the pandemic once they reached the end of the tunnel, it was important that users scrolled through the tunnel as quickly as possible.

11

Less is more.

We're finally here at the biggest design debate and cliché of the twentieth century—less is more. Every year I have my students debate various design clichés, and less is more is always the most controversial. Before hearing both sides of the argument, students tend to believe that less is more, but afterwards, almost all of them change their minds. The truth is, there is no right or wrong here. Sometimes less is more, and sometimes it's not. Later on we'll cover the other side of this argument (see Principle 12), but let's first look at when less actually is more in UX.

The phrase comes from midcentury architecture and was popularized in 1947 by German modernist architect Ludwig Mies van der Rohe who—like other people associated with the Bauhaus—argued that elegance did not derive from abundance and that less decoration had more impact than a lot. The famous quote was a direct reaction against the overly ornate architectural style of the nineteenth century and ushered in the rational, minimalist, and functionalist architecture movement of the twentieth century.

So how does this apply to UX? According to Australian educational psychologist John Sweller, overloading our memory typically results in a higher rate of errors. So less is more when interfaces require us to perform complicated tasks. If I need to fill out my taxes or apply for healthcare online, less is definitely more.

When we were working on the ticket purchasing flow of the new M+ museum in Hong Kong, we very carefully thought about making it as simple and error-proof as possible. When M+ delivered the functional requirements to us, we insisted on stripping away all functionality that did not immediately help the user complete their task and lobbied against adding promotional messaging. We proposed a very clear, minimalist, hyperfunctional, and bare-bones interface that would not burden the user's cognitive load and would leave no space for interpretation.

This was in stark contrast to the maximalist approach we took in other parts of the M+ digital experience, which was deliberately ornamental and full of personality. Other parts of the interface were meant to inspire, generate a sense of wonder and amazement, and entice people to come visit the museum. It did not require the user to perform any kind of complicated task.

There is a place for ornate design and maximalism in UX. But when it comes to complicated tasks or processes, less is more. If we strip away all the unnecessary and reduce the operational and cognitive costs, we greatly improve the design's usability and are left with the bare minimum required to make complicated interactions easier.

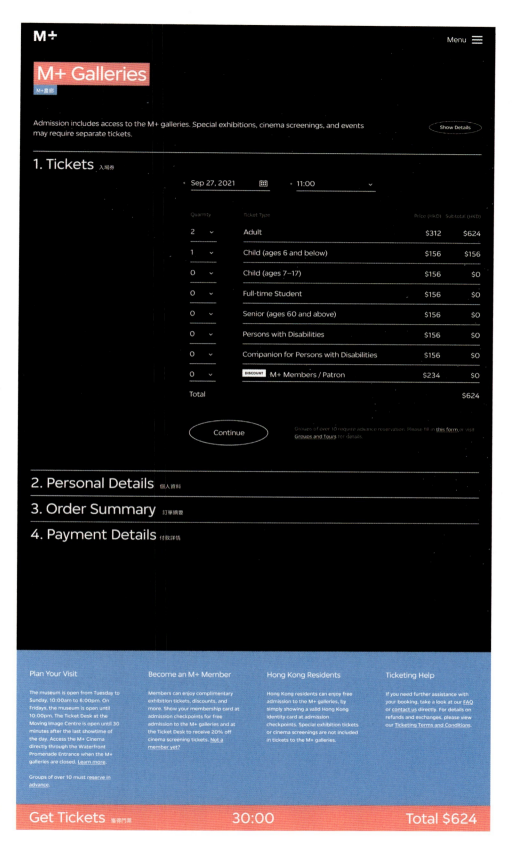

→
We deliberately made the ticket-purchasing process for the new M+ museum in Hong Kong as simple and straightforward as possible, creating an easy-to-understand, step-by-step process that would eliminate the potential for errors.

12

Less is a bore.

Twenty years after the rational tyranny of Mies van der Rohe's "less is more" (see Principle 11), the architect Robert Venturi coined the phrase "less is a bore." The phrase was meant to criticize the prevailing minimalist and functionalist modernist architectural movement, instead celebrating the highly stylized and decorative designs of classical architectural movements that came before. It argued for personality and maximalism.

In the early days of web design, there was still quite a bit of personality and experimentation, but we slowly started to lose that in the early 2000s when we realized that users performed better on complicated tasks when anything unnecessary is stripped away. But rather than using a minimalist approach only when we needed to lower the cognitive load, we started applying it everywhere.

That's a problem. Open up any website or app that was made in the past ten years and you'll see they almost all look the same. This bland Bauhaus-era of UX design is easy to replicate, doesn't require a whole lot of skill, and has no personality. Swap out the logo on any of these minimalist websites and try to guess which company it is. Good luck.

The good thing is that when everything looks the same, we can grab attention by simply being different. That's where maximalism comes in; it has the power to evoke different sensations and emotions through loud color combinations, contrasting patterns, multiple font pairings, and unusual interaction models. It's the antidote to the sameness of minimalist design.

When working on the website of the noncommercial adaptation of Peter Watts science fiction novel *Blindsight*, my partner, Anton—who is in charge of UI design at our studio—dialed up the maximalism to the max. The navigation was in a spiral, the side-scrolling inside the chapters was strange, and combining PX Grotesk with Begum (a technical typeface with a Roman serif) created an uneasy type clash. And yet it functioned. That's because great care was put into testing all the interactions to make sure the user wouldn't be hindered by the design.

If a design is difficult to use, it's neither maximalist or minimalist—it's just bad. Maximalism is not about cluttering the screen with a bunch of stuff just for the sake of it. The design still has to function. If minimalism is like a gray office building, maximalism is like a kindergarten building in the shape of a cat. It's not about adding ornamentation for the sake of it.

↓
Key screens from the *Blindsight* interactive experience, an adaptation of the eponymous science fiction novel by Peter Watts. The inspiration for the futuristic art direction and spiral interaction model came from the book in which the main character records all of his memories while on his voyage back to Earth.

13

Provide feedback quickly or else.

It's not often that UX gets glamorized in fiction, but in an episode of the television show *Halt and Catch Fire* (which is about the personal computer revolution of the 1980s), an urban legend was born: "You ask your computer to do something and hit the enter key; if it answers you back in less than 400 milliseconds, just under half a second, then you will stay glued to that machine for hours. Your eyes may glaze over, but your productivity will soar. You'll be transfixed, mesmerized. Even a slight deviation back to half a second response time will allow your attention to stray. You'll get up and do the dishes, pick up the remote, and watch the game. But under 400 milliseconds, ah, that's the sweet spot."

These magical 0.4 seconds of response time is actually an oversimplification of a totally different theory published in a 1982 IBM research paper by Walter J. Doherty et al., which had nothing to do with making people more addicted to an interface but with optimizing their programmers' productivity. It concluded that productivity increases when a computer and a user interact at a pace that ensures neither has to wait on the other. And the faster the response time, the higher the programmer's productivity, resulting in more money saved or made in the long run.

But let's break down the actual numbers as they relate to websites and apps today, not the productivity of IBM programmers in the early 1980s. According to human-computer interaction researcher Jakob Nielsen, there are three important response-time thresholds to keep in mind when designing:

- 0.1 seconds is the limit for feeling that the system is reacting instantaneously.
- 1 second is the limit for the user's flow of thought to stay uninterrupted, even though the user will notice the delay.
- 10 seconds is the limit for keeping attention focused on the ongoing interaction.

What that means is that if a computer responds to our input in less than a second, we think of it as a responsive system, but if we have to wait more than a second for the computer to respond, we think of it as slow. So as designers, after about two seconds, we should notify the user that the computer is "thinking," and after about five seconds, we already want to start letting people know how much more time they're going to have to wait.

Why? Because speed is the ultimate usability metric. It has such an impact on our experience that it can become the one thing people will remember most, making it even more memorable than the actual design. In other words, ugly but fast is better than pretty but slow. But not always. Sometimes it's actually good to slow people down a little (see Principle 14).

→
For the online collection of Hong Kong's M+ museum, the endless scroll allows users to see all the artwork that is in the museum's collection. When users scroll too fast—or their internet connection is slow—the system notifies them that more content is still loading.

M+

Wucius Wong
Elevation
1973

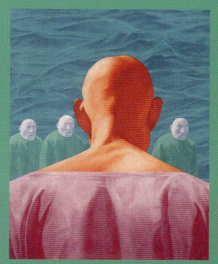

Fang Lijun
Untitled
1995

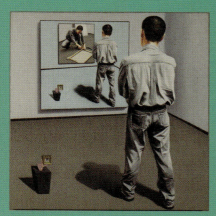

Fang Lijun
Untitled
1995

Firenze Lai
The Bone Setting Clinic
2012

Guang Tingbo
I Graze Horse for My Motherland
1973

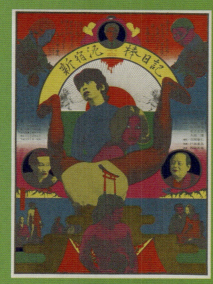

Yokoo Tadanori
Diary of a Shinjuku Burglar
1968

Zhang Xiaogang
Bloodline Series- Big Family No.
17-1998
1998

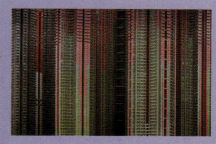

Michael Wolf
Architecture of Density, No.39
2005

Zhang Hongzan
Settle down in where the oil was
found
1973

Yue Minjun
2000 A.D. (Group of sculptures. 25
figures)
2000

Loading More Items

14

Friction isn't always bad.

It's our job to make things as easy as possible, remove all obstacles for the user, and design the experience so they can accomplish their goal in the fastest way possible, right? Well, not always. While unwanted friction should always be eliminated, not all interactions require the speed of a frictionless experience. Sometimes we actually need users to slow down and focus on what they are about to do, especially when there are serious consequences to their actions.

Every time we're asked "Are you sure you want to delete this?," "Do you consent to our cookie policy?," or "Did you mean to send an email without a subject?," we're interacting with a deliberately designed case of friction.

The problem is that we tend to swat these pop-ups away like annoying flies without really reading them. A 2010 HCI study by Böhme and Köpsell showed that over 50 percent of users do not read end-user license agreements and will click whatever affirmative button to continue with what they're doing. That's fine if you're mindlessly accepting cookie pop-ups and aren't super concerned about your privacy (you should be), but when you wake up on New Year's Day and realize you were just charged $350 for your fifteen-minute ride home the night before, it's a serious problem.

Before ride-sharing app Uber added friction to their price-surge acceptance screen, most people would mindlessly accept many more times the price of the original fare. This frictionless experience led to extremely annoyed customers and an F rating (the lowest possible) from the Better Business Bureau.

To counteract this, Uber introduced a deliberate moment of friction: For example, if the current surge price is 3.25 times the normal fare, users have to manually type "3 2 5" to confirm. This patented method of forcing users to manually agree made people hyperaware of what they were actually agreeing to and drastically improved customer satisfaction.

Yes, unwanted friction is bad (see Principle 13). But sometimes a little friction is a good thing. Since everything we design has a tangible effect on society and people's lives, it's up to individual designers to not exploit people's inertia and uphold standards of security and safety. Whether that means getting people out of autopilot mode, preventing them from making unintended decisions or errors, creating engaging challenges in games, or enhancing security, friction helps people pause and make more deliberate decisions.

15

First impressions matter.

An impression is made in the blink of an eye—or ten seconds. From research done at Microsoft by Chao Liu, Ryen W. White, and Susan Dumais, we know that if users don't see or understand the value of a web page within ten seconds, they'll leave. That's because users know that they will easily be able to find whatever it is that they need somewhere else. Ten seconds is all we get to make a first impression and convince people to stay.

So what constitutes a good first impression? Surprisingly it's not the content. It's the design. People tend to mistrust digital products that are poorly designed. If people don't like the layout, typography, imagery, and color schemes at first glance, they won't care about the content and will almost never explore any further (see Principle 8). So the first impression is extremely important. But to understand where to focus our attention, we first need to understand where the majority of our visitors start their experience.

When the British artist Shantell Martin reached out in need of a new brand and website, we spent quite a bit of time discussing how we can best represent her online. Since we knew from looking at her current website analytics that the highest number of people start exploring her website through her homepage, we focused most of our attention there. And to stop people in their tracks, we thought of her homepage not as a homepage but as a movie poster—or a book cover, or packaging. Things that are deliberately designed to draw attention.

We selected an extremely bold typeface that would contrast with the ephemeral and hand-drawn nature of her art, and led with an oversized image of her lying on top of her work. Since her art often invites the viewer to participate, we used interactivity so visitors can interact with her work just like in real life. People loved it and ended up spending an unusually high amount of time on her homepage.

Great design not only gets people to trust you, it's what makes them want to stick around. And since we know we only get ten seconds to make a first impression, they should count. So before we open the door, let's make sure our house is in order, we have our best outfit on, and there's nothing between our teeth, and welcome people with a smile.

Early on in the concepting phase for Shantell Martin's new brand and website, we came up with the "body of work" concept, where the interaction model is represented by her physical body. The inspiration for the photograph of her lying on top of her work came from Annie Leibovitz's striking portrait of Keith Haring where he—along with the room he is in—is covered in his work.

16

UX design isn't timeless.

German industrial designer Dieter Rams famous for elevating Braun's product lineup into something covetable and inspirational (some even say Apple's Jonathan Ive may have copied Ram's designs a little too closely when designing the first iPod), developed the often quoted "10 Principles of Good Design" in the 1970s. According to Rams, good design:

Is innovative
Makes a product useful
Is aesthetic
Makes a product understandable
Is unobtrusive
Is honest
Is long lasting
Is thorough down to the last detail
Is environmentally friendly
Involves as little design as possible

In the context of industrial design, architecture, or even graphic design, I tend to agree with this list. When it comes to UX design, however, there is one item here that doesn't apply: Good UX design is not long lasting. The field and practice itself is long lasting, but there really is no such thing as timeless design when it comes to interfaces.

Why? Because how we interact with computers is very dependent on the software and hardware technology available in that particular moment in history. Just take something as simple as the mouse. Though it was first invented in the early 1960s by SRI's Douglas Engelbart, it didn't become commercially available until 1984. Or take the touchscreen, which was invented by Eric A. Johnson in 1965 but didn't become widely accepted until the 2000s.

And that's just the hardware. Programming languages and browser technologies are also continuously evolving. If we would have put a hamburger menu (the little three stripes icon that opens the navigation on a mobile device) in front of a person twenty years ago, they probably wouldn't have known what to do with it (see Principle 82).

With technology constantly evolving, the average interface has a maximum shelf life of about twenty years, and that number is getting shorter and shorter as technological advancements accelerate each year. An interface will always be a product of its time. But the good news is that we as humans evolve as well. Whenever something new is introduced, we learn and adapt, making space for even more advancements in how we interact with computers. So we don't need UX to be timeless.

17

Nothing lasts forever.

Out of the over 100 client projects Anton and I have worked on together over the past fifteen years, we can very easily categorize them into two groups: those that are still exactly how we designed them (sigh of relief), and those that have completely changed (RIP). And it has nothing to do with the timelessness of the design, the evolution of technology, or the quality of the work. It has to do with who is in charge on the client side and how high their turnover rate is.

Most digitally native products are still founder owned (Craigslist, Google/Alphabet, Facebook/Meta, and Spotify, to name a few), and they tend to value longevity over fads. They know frequent changes make users nervous and apprehensive about accidentally doing something wrong, and the last thing they want to do is alienate their current user base. Despite having hundreds of designers in-house (see Principle 85), design changes are introduced sparingly, and interfaces stay more or less the same year after year.

The opposite is true when we work for clients whose products are not digitally native. Design changes are frequent and oftentimes decided by whoever happens to be in charge at that moment. This person may or may not be very familiar with digital and probably thinks they are doing users a favor by continuously messing with the interface. Or maybe they just don't think about their users at all. Whatever the case, every new team that comes in wants to put their stamp on the product, bring in their people, and redesign everything.

Just as royals rule for lifetimes and elected officials are always struggling to win the next election, the longevity of a design in digital is guarded by whomever commissioned the work. And if the people on the client side keep changing (most people in the United States only stay at a job for an average of three years), the likelihood of a design remaining the same, even just for five years, is slim to none.

The only reason some of our projects are still exactly how we designed them is that they are carefully guarded by the same leadership team who initiated the work in the first place. But we know that as soon as they leave and a new team comes in, we have to be prepared to say a little prayer and bid farewell to our work. It's OK. I've gotten used to it. I used to think of our past projects as my babies, but I now think of them more as my ex-husbands.

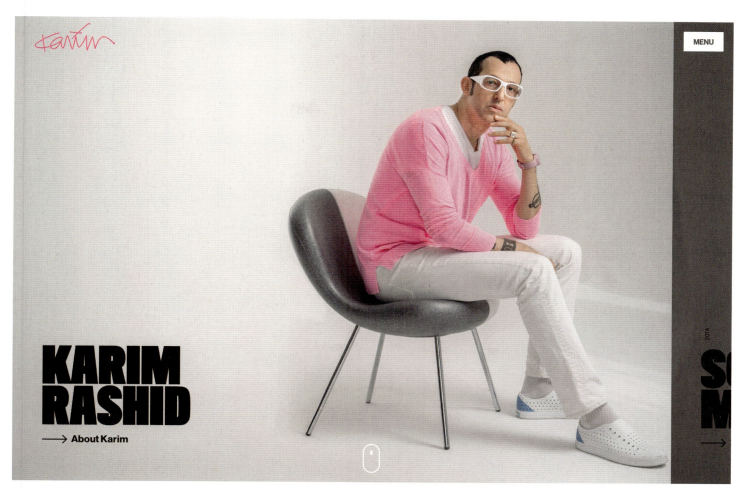

↑
One of our longest-lasting projects is the website for designer Karim Rashid. As of the time of this writing, the website has been live and unchanged for over nine years. That's because Karim Rashid was the one who commissioned the work and is obviously still at the helm of his eponymous studio.

We can design experiences th people, or we c to deliberately coerce for pers

meaningful
help
n choose
nislead and
nal gain.

18

Accessibility first.

Accessibility in UX is usability for people who interact with products differently. That could mean people who are blind or color blind or people with mobility, hearing, or learning difficulties, but it also includes people who are sleep deprived, intoxicated, holding a baby while also holding a mobile phone, or people who need their glasses to read.

Accessibility is essential for some, but it's useful for all of us. If accessibility is considered up front and implemented correctly, it ends up benefiting everyone. Consider these examples:

- Closed captions on videos are essential for people who are deaf but are also helpful for people who are watching the video in public.
- Upping the contrast is essential for people who are visually impaired, but it's also helpful for people who are using their phones in glaring sunlight.
- Simplifying language is essential for people with learning disabilities, but it's also helpful for people whose native language is not English.
- Keyboard-only navigation is vital for people with motor impairments, but it's also helpful for people whose mouse just broke.

And the list goes on and on. Since it benefits everyone, you'd think all digital products are designed to be accessible, right? Wrong. A 2020 report by WebAIM states that only 2 percent of the most widely used websites meet accessibility standards. With no regulations forcing private companies to ensure their products are accessible, it's often not even a consideration.

But there's hope. Since 1998, thanks to the Americans with Disabilities Act (ADA), government websites in the United States are required and expected to ensure all of their digital content is accessible under Section 508. To facilitate that process, the World Wide Web Consortium (W3C) offers free tools to educate designers on how to develop accessible products and checks to validate that they are.

Europe is going even a step further. The European Accessibility Act will be the first standardized directive applied specifically to the private sector in Europe. These regulations will go into effect in 2025 and will be applicable to all private companies of ten people or more or whose annual balance sheet exceeds 2 million euros.

However, making a product accessible is not the sole responsibility of the designer. Ensuring that website copy can be read out loud to a visually impaired person, for example, is achieved through code, not design. Developers need to ensure that all the code, markup, and libraries they select result in accessible design, and UX designers need to educate their clients on its benefits and lobby for its implementation (see Principle 65). The more we design with accessibility in mind, the better the results are for everybody.

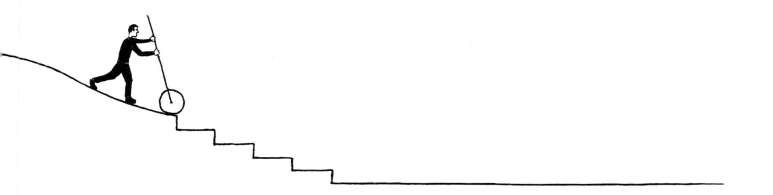

19

Allow for differences in digital literacy.

Not knowing how to read or write makes it nearly impossible to succeed in society. But in today's world, where almost everything—including banking, booking vaccination appointments, and paying taxes—happens digitally, literacy goes beyond the basic ability to comprehend text. It now includes the skills and knowledge necessary to be able to evaluate, use, and create many different kinds of digital information, content, and tools.

In 2001, education consultant Marc Prensky popularized the terms "digital native" and "digital immigrant." Generally speaking, digital immigrants grew up in a non-digital, pre-internet culture, and digital natives were born after the world was fully digitized. (Millennials are considered to be the oldest generation of digital natives.) However, digital literacy is not strictly divided by generational lines. People of any age who've had little to no access to the internet are also considered digital immigrants.

So how does this affect the way we approach the design of a product? Typically, when we design interfaces that are meant to be used by people with varying levels of digital literacy (for example, an interface for hospital administrators or a website for a museum), we need to make sure that the design of the interface can be used easily regardless of digital literacy. That means designing for the people with the lowest level of digital literacy first.

The North Star should be to minimize any potential for fear or confusion. This looks like ensuring that the interactions and language are easily understood and context-appropriate, people are able to go at their own pace, and the design team spends extra effort making sure there is sufficient help and instructional information throughout the experience.

Memory aids that show the relationships between categories (like color coding) and flexible learning pathways that offer an entry level into usage can also ambiently educate users on more complex parts of the interface in a scaffolded way. And if we know that people with lower digital literacy are responsible for entering data, the system itself can be designed in a way to ensure quality control.

If we follow these guidelines when we know our tools will also be used by people with lower digital literacy, it will make them more comfortable interacting with technology in general. And as they use more apps and services, their skills will improve and their confidence will increase, making it easier for them to exist in today's digital world.

Empathize

20

Take extra care of seniors.

A lot of the difficulties seniors face when dealing with digital products have to do with the fact that they were introduced to new technologies later in life—they're digital immigrants (see Principle 19). This makes some seniors insecure when dealing with a new digital product for the first time.

When we were working on the redesign of the Met Museum's website, we knew that a large part of the audience would be over sixty-five, so we had to take extra care in thinking through how to ensure seniors could confidently use our interface.

In general seniors need a bit more time to absorb the information on an interface. They tend to carefully review all the elements on the screen before taking action and take instructional copy very literally. It was important that the copy wasn't in any way ambiguous and that processes like purchasing tickets were easy to understand and didn't make them feel rushed.

Besides removing all unnecessary elements and making everything bigger, we also decided to minimize the number of icons used across the interface. For people who haven't spent a whole lot of time online, icons are not as universally understood as you might think (see Principle 82). Clear labels, however, can be understood by everyone. So we decided on a design system that led with words.

We also lobbied against forcing people to create an account, because for some seniors, entering passwords can create a slight panic. We made sure all people (not just seniors) were able to interact with all of the Met's content—including purchasing tickets or making donations—without ever having to create an account.

Though future generations who did grow up with digital technology will probably not face these exact same challenges once they are over sixty-five, these considerations are not exclusive to today's seniors. If we design something that seniors can confidently use, other digital immigrants will find it much easier to interact as well.

→
Key screens from the Met Museum's website across desktop, mobile, and tablet showcase a bold and oversized UI that was specifically designed to be as easy to use as possible by people across all demographics, but especially seniors.

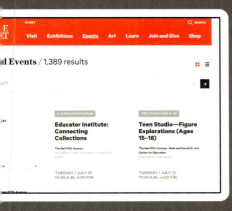

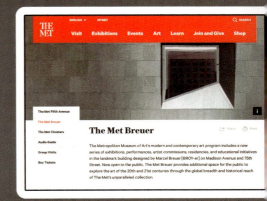
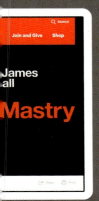

21

Children are not small adults.

When we were working on the first iPad app for Nickelodeon—a children's television network—we instinctively knew that an interface that works great for most people might not work at all for kids. It was the first time we were designing something for children, and we didn't want to insult their intelligence by simply dumbing down the interface or slapping some bright colors and cartoon characters on the screen and calling it a day.

During one of the usability studies, the kids were given iPads so we could observe their content-discovery process. Whereas adults tend to stick to the main path when trying to find information, we discovered that children actually like to try many different options. One kid was typing random letters—like the letter *F*—into the YouTube search bar and hitting enter. When asked why, he answered, "I just wanted to see what would happen."

Unlike adults, who can easily be placed in broad age groups like twenty-five to forty-five, defining the right age groups for children is much more critical, as not all children's developmental stages are the same. The Nick app had to appeal to children between the ages of six to eleven, which put our app more or less in the "concrete operational stage" as theorized by child development psychologist Jean Piaget. And since the aim of this stage is to develop logical thought processes and learn about how things work, we looked at number games, logic games, crosswords puzzles, and STEM toys for inspiration.

We went to work designing an interface that would require quite a bit of effort for children to figure out. Rather than making it easy, we deliberately made it hard (see Principle 46). To find the exact thing they were looking for, kids had to swipe and pan around this giant imaginary table that held all the content. If they closed and opened the app again, all the content would reshuffle. So to find the same thing again, they had to figure out the underlying logic of the system. To add a little bit of fun to the exploration, we added some "DO NOT TOUCH" buttons here and there, which would cover the entire screen in Nickelodeon's green slime if tapped.

When we launched the app, we were a bit nervous. Would kids get it? All the adults we showed it to seemed skeptical. When it became the most downloaded free entertainment app on the App Store and won an Emmy Award a year later (we had no idea apps could even win Emmys), we knew the gamble had paid off. Kids loved it. By celebrating how children between the ages of six to eleven interact with content differently than we do, we managed to create an experience that respected the spirit of childhood.

22

Design for learnability.

The term "learnability" in UX design refers to how easy it is to interact with a new product and the degree of effort required to learn to perform new tasks. It's a form of usability, except that when designing for learnability, we have to take into account that the user will probably have to learn how to use the interface while interacting with it. When learnability is high, users are able to learn novel interactions without any training or instructions.

Some interfaces have higher learning curves than others. Standard websites like booking platforms or e-commerce sites will not have much of a learning curve at all. But more complicated computer games or specific technology applications make users only more proficient with each subsequent use.

Whenever we design an interface that requires high learnability, we always look at computer games for inspiration. Game designers are extremely good at teaching complexity and giving the right kind of feedback at the right time so people aren't even really aware they are learning something new.

When we were working on our interactive documentary *One Shared House*, we took inspiration from early video games that combined storytelling with interactions, like *Where in the World Is Carmen Sandiego?*. Users could simply watch the film from start to finish—like any other video on the internet—or they could click on the interactive elements that would appear at the bottom of the screen to get more background information on specific topics mentioned throughout the film.

This is a very uncommon way to interact with content online, so we looked at how quickly users were able to figure it out for the first time, how quickly they got better with each repeated visit, and how easy it was to use once they figured it out completely.

The goal for any complex product, or any product that introduces novel interactions, is to minimize the effort required to become an experienced user (see Principle 19). If you come up with something that users have likely not encountered before, don't be alarmed if the initial usability isn't high right off the bat. Worry instead about designing a system that allows users to ambiently learn it while interacting with it.

→
Key screens from our self-produced interactive documentary *One Shared House*, about my experience growing up in a communal house in the center of Amsterdam. Each scene came with additional content users would be able to explore by tapping on some of the contextual questions that would appear throughout the film, or viewers could choose to simply watch the documentary sequentially.

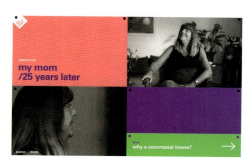

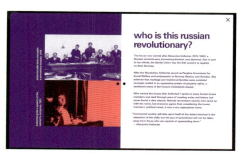

Empathize

23

Don't just design for novices.

Most of the time when we're in the early stages of discussing what the interface should be, we tend to focus on first-time visitors. We design a welcome experience that is easy to understand and quick to use and create onboarding screens that help people get familiar with the interface (see Principle 15). But that's only half the work.

What happens when users return frequently? Or are experts at using the product and already know their way around all the corners of the interface? Those types of people don't need us to hold their hand. They need faster speed and greater control to perform more sophisticated tasks.

These types of users are called power users, and almost every product has them. But only features that will be used frequently—or actions that require greater control— need to be designed for power use. And to help clarify the exact additional features required, it's important to understand where power users differ and how they might use the interface to perform more complex tasks.

Maybe it's all about speed, and we need to consider keyboard shortcuts. Or maybe they need to batch execute tasks, and we need to create macros. Or maybe they need to configure more complicated settings, and we need to provide an advanced control panel. Whatever the case may be, as soon as a product is used by someone on a daily basis, they're going to need more advanced features designed with frequent use in mind.

Whenever we create a content management system for a client (an internal tool that allows them to create, edit, and publish content), we have to make sure the interface is welcoming to both novice editors, who will probably use only the basic features to upload or change something every once in a while, as well as daily power users, who need to frequently batch upload multiple changes at once or schedule updates for a specific time.

Almost all products need both a "novice" and an "expert" mode, but it's important to keep in mind that power user features should always be an alternative way to use the interface—never the primary way. Advanced features should be tucked away by default and easy to ignore. But when they're needed, they should also be just as easy to find.

→
The CMS (content management system) we designed for the Spotify design team allowed a select group of people within Spotify to publish content on the Spotify website without having to involve any designers or developers. They could create gradients that would support the header of the page and add content in any order they wanted through the use of formatted text, images, galleries, videos, quotes, and downloads, as well as embedded code, widgets, and Spotify music players.

Universal Principles of UX

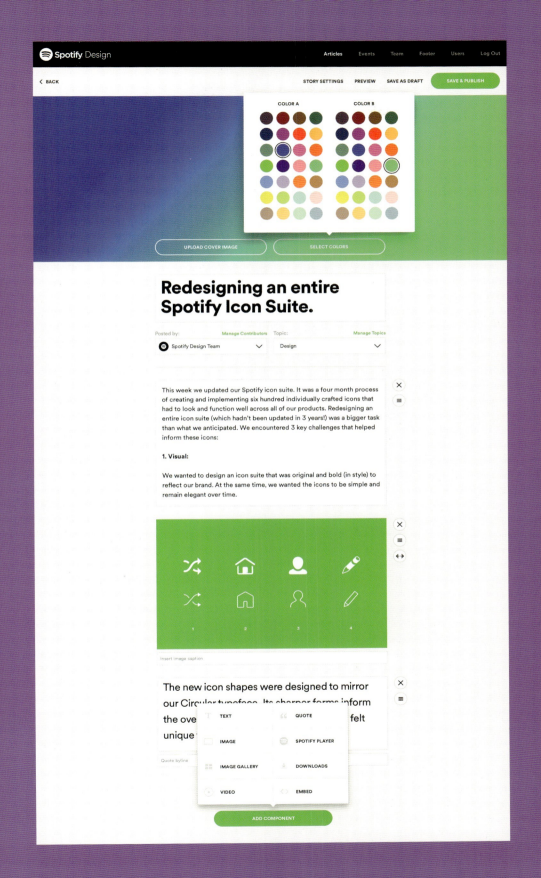

24

Make the choice easy.

The first time I walked through a supermarket in Atlanta, Georgia, I felt paralyzed. Being from the Netherlands, I was not used to seeing such an overwhelming number of options for cereal, jam, cheese, or toilet paper. I must have spent at least an hour trying to figure out what cheese to buy. Choice is good, but too much choice stresses us out and prolongs our decision-making process.

This psychological phenomenon is referred to as Hick's law, named after early 1950s experimentations around choice by psychologists William Edmund Hick and Ray Hyman. It applies to situations in which decisions are actually not that important (like me choosing the right cheese), but it doesn't apply to decisions that carry heavier consequences (like choosing between universities or job offers). In other words, it's more stressful to have many options when the choice is frivolous than when the choice matters.

When it comes to designing interfaces, it is extremely important to not overwhelm people with a bunch of unimportant options and present them with only the choices that matter.

A couple of years ago, the music streaming provider Spotify asked us to help create the interface for an internal research tool. They had spent three years gathering incredibly in-depth, actionable insights around why, how, and when people listen to music together, but to their dismay, nobody was utilizing it. And not surprisingly. They had put all the research in incredibly overwhelming spreadsheets that were so impenetrable that whoever dared to open them would immediately regret it.

To get the right depth of research to the right person in the quickest way possible, we went through all the spreadsheets line by line. We categorized and organized all the research in such a way that the new interface required only four questions to get to relevant information. A process that used to take hours (if people even followed through with it at all) could now be accomplished in ten seconds or less (see Principle 15), resulting in many more people accessing and utilizing the research within Spotify.

Hick's law is extremely important in UX. The worst digital products are universally characterized as having too many choices and options. When designing interfaces, it's important to create a system that will do most of the heavy lifting and smartly cut out the largest number of frivolous or unimportant options for the user. UX designers are responsible for organizing content in such a way that users are left with only the choices that actually matter.

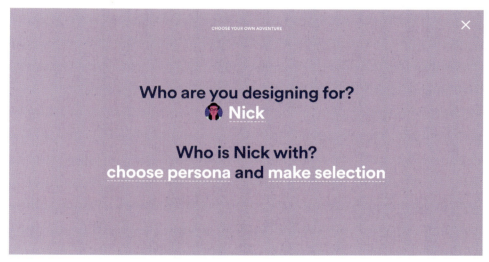

→
For the interactive research tool we worked on for Spotify, which was meant to display Spotify's research on people's preferences around listening to music together, we created an interface that allowed people within Spotify to quickly filter through all the data through conversational language. In 10 seconds or less, people were able to get to actionable insights that they could take into their product definition or design process.

25

Diverse teams create better solutions.

Design is run by white men. To be exact, 76 percent of people who design for the web are white, and 58 percent of them are men. That obviously is not representative of our society and leads to bias issues.

When Apple's voice assistant Siri was first introduced in 2011, I remember thinking how sexist it was to make an obedient, submissive, compliant, personal assistant *female*. But with only 22 percent of jobs in artificial intelligence being held by women, I imagine that there probably weren't enough female voices in the room to offer an alternative perspective.

Alternative perspectives are an advantage. According to research by social scientists Lu Hong and Scott E. Page, teams with differences in demographics, cultural identities, ethnicity, training, and expertise find better solutions to complex problems than homogeneous teams. That's because people with different experiences solve problems differently, and that diversity outperforms the problem solving of homogeneous groups.

Diverse teams are also better for the bottom line. A 2015 McKinsey report on 366 public companies found that companies in the top quartile for racial and ethnic diversity are 35 percent more likely to have financial returns above their respective national industry medians. And that's big money.

But most importantly, when a diverse group of people comes together, they're more likely to question their own assumptions, consider the needs and wants of different kinds of people, and challenge what they consider "normal" or "standard," and less likely to gender code or stereotype. In other words, they're more likely to be less biased.

Why should we care? Because history has taught us that what is acceptable today could be inconsiderate, hurtful, or discriminatory tomorrow. That's why it's important to surround ourselves with people who are different from us and keep different types of people top of mind throughout the entire design process.

As UX designers, we are shaping what the digital world looks like. Let's keep our biases in check and question our own assumptions. If we make sure that what we release into the world is more representative and respectful of our shared diversity, everyone wins.

26

Context matters more than screen size.

In 2007, the year that both the iPhone and smart TVs were introduced, Nokia's cultural anthropologist Jan Chipchase released research revealing that three items were now considered essential across all cultures and genders: keys, money, and a mobile phone. This meant that designing mobile interfaces could no longer be an afterthought.

While we were working on the website redesign of *USA Today* in 2012, Apple introduced the iPad, so our design system had to work across three different screen sizes and ratios (desktop, mobile, and tablet). But screen size was only half the battle. The most important thing we had to think about was each device's unique context of use. Because *when* we use certain devices and *why* is far more important than screen size (see Principle 84).

We dove into the website's analytics and dissected *USA Today*'s incoming traffic per device, which revealed a clear, predictable pattern. Smartphones dominated the morning and evening commute time, desktop browsers accounted for the highest amount of traffic during standard working hours, and tablets became a bigger player later in the evening.

Since on mobile devices we are more likely to be on the go and switching between different applications, the mobile layout needed to support stop-and-go consumption. That meant large headlines with short sections, as well as strong enough contrast that could easily be seen in glaring sunlight. And since we had to account for single-handed use—thumbs can only stretch so far—we put the most frequently used elements at the bottom of the interface.

Though initially intended as mobile devices, tablets tend to stay in the home and are predominantly used for entertainment and long-form content. So the typeface and type size in the long-form articles on tablets had to account for reading comfort first, and the layout had to work equally well in vertical and horizontal orientations.

When, where, why, and how we access content needs to be considered well before we actually start designing anything, because when it comes to designing for multiple devices, there is no one-size-fits-all solution. When a system is designed for context of use rather than screen size, there is a higher chance that the interface will be more appropriate and feel more comfortable.

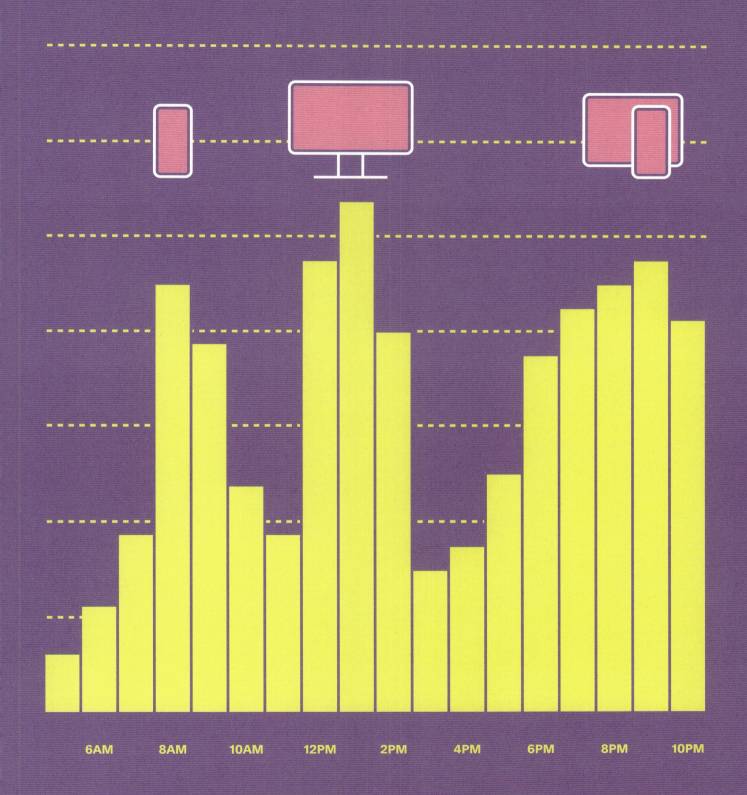

27

Design for clumsy handling.

Have you ever seen a toddler interact with a tablet? Or a cat? When I gave my baby boomer mother her first iPad in 2012 (her first home computer ever), I was amazed at how intuitively she was able to interact with it. Even complicated tasks—like changing the system language from English to Dutch—she figured out on her own without any involvement from me.

The founder of Fantasy Interactive, where I worked early on in my career, always used to tell us to make all of our designs and interactions feel like Fisher-Price (the oversized toddler toys). What he meant was that we should take cues from the tangibility and high usability of toddler toys and make everything bigger. If it's bigger, it's automatically easier to use.

One of the reasons tablets are so intuitive is that when we design for touch, we have to make sure that the tappable area of each button, menu item, or link is roughly the size of a normal human fingertip, key on a keyboard, or button on a remote control. That is not the case when designing for mouse inputs, which can target much smaller areas (see Principle 51).

A 2003 MIT study that investigated the mechanics of tactile sense found that the average human fingertip is between 8 to 10 millimeters. And when it comes to interface design, both Apple and Android recommend a touch target size of 7 to 10 millimeters, with a 5-millimeter separation between interactive elements to ensure people don't accidentally tap the wrong item.

These are just recommendations, however. Someone once told me the story of how they designed a mobile app to help power-grid repairmen log issues. The app had all the required functionality, but the repairmen found the interface hard to use. The designers invited the repairmen over for some usability testing, and as soon as they walked in, the problem was immediately clear: These repairmen's hands were much bigger than the average person's hand.

Regardless of what we are designing, if buttons are bigger, options are fewer, and contrast is higher by default, we can accommodate a larger spectrum of users without much effort. We can make sure our products can be used by children, seniors, people with motor or vision impairments, cats, or even power-grid repairmen with unusually large hands.

↑
Our self-initiated x100 is a simple iOS app that allows people to easily keep track of their reps during workouts. Since we wanted to make sure that people were able to focus on their workout—and are likely quite sweaty—we made sure that all interactive elements were as big and bulky as possible.

28

Match the
real world.

Whenever we have to come up with a new interface for a project, we always start by thinking about how people would interact with it in the real world. That way it feels familiar and people immediately know what to do. It's also why we delete things by dragging it to the trash, group documents into folders, and use the compass, flashlight, calculator, and clock on our phones without any instruction.

During the concepting phase of *USA Today*, rather than looking at other newspaper websites for inspiration, we closely examined the actual physical newspaper and talked about what our behavior is like when reading newspapers. People don't tend to read the newspaper from start to finish like a book. Most of us will scan the front page for interesting articles and then dive into our favorite sections.

For example, I always start with international politics, then move on to science, then art, and then (if I don't put it in the recycling bin at that point) I might read more articles in other sections. That's why the newspaper is folded to make it easy to take out *your* favorite section, while someone else in the household can easily take out *their* favorite section.

USA Today color codes all of its individual sections. They also drive articles with large headlines and have a much bigger emphasis on imagery. Besides keeping all of those design elements intact, we also created an interaction model that made it easier for users to stay within their preferred section, much like how they would if reading a physical newspaper.

Almost everything we design as an interface can be found in the real world, and we already have an expectation of how we are supposed to interact with it (see Principle 62). Instead of looking at other websites for inspiration, we always take cues from the analog version of whatever it is we are designing. Because if the interaction model and the design elements we select for the UI have some sort of parallel to the real world, the interface will feel familiar, making it much more likely that people will understand how to use it right away.

↓
On the left side is Wolff Olins's redesign of *USA Today*'s physical newspaper from 2012, and on the right side is the final UI of the digital newspaper we worked on simultaneously.

Empathize

29

Know when to break with convention.

In 2000, human-computer interaction researcher Jakob Nielsen stated that since users spend most of their time on various sites, they prefer sites to work the same as all the other sites they already know. So according to Nielsen, as designers we have a responsibility to adhere to people's expectations, make all interfaces standardized, and follow conventions at all times.

No thanks. I don't want to live in a world where every single website looks the same. And with audiences having gotten a whole lot more sophisticated since Jakob Nielsen first made that statement back in 2000, there are many examples of how breaking with interface conventions not only works, but also leads to higher engagement.

When Sundar Pichai was heading up the Google Chrome team in 2010 (before he was promoted to CEO of Alphabet), we worked with his team on the "20 Things I Learned about Browsers and the Web" interactive experience. The Google Chrome team had written twenty "things" to help people better understand some core web concepts, and Christoph Niemann was tapped to create illustrations.

Rather than making it look like a standard website, we wanted the articles to feel more important, almost like Google had written a thesis. We settled on making the interface look like an actual book. There was a cover that opened to reveal a spread, and users could manually flip through the pages horizontally. It also worked in offline mode, so if users would leave and come back, there would be a little bookmark indicating where they last left off.

The project was hugely successful, engagement was much higher than anticipated, and the UX and visual design was honored at the 2012 Webby Awards. It looked like no other website out there at the time. It broke with all conventions. Jakob Nielsen would have hated it.

Breaking with convention can be a good thing, but it has to be a deliberate act and should never be done accidentally or out of ignorance of the norm. It should also always take the intended target audience into consideration. But if we do manage to create something new that is still very intuitive to use, people will not only interact with it easily, but they'll probably remember it much more favorably as well (see Principle 9).

↓
Key screens from the "20 Things I Learned about Browsers and the Web" interactive experience we worked on for Google in 2010.

30

Persuade, don't coerce.

In 1971 designer Victor Papanek said, "There are professions more harmful than industrial design, but only a very few of them. And possibly only one profession is phonier. Advertising design, in persuading people to buy things they don't need, with money they don't have, in order to impress others who don't care, is probably the phoniest field in existence today. Industrial design, by concocting the tawdry idiocies hawked by advertisers, comes a close second."

If advertising comes first and industrial design comes second, then UX design definitely comes third. Though we claim to be the advocate for the user, we are more often than not actually serving as the advocate for the sales or marketing team. We observe how people behave, and by using pretty rudimentary psychological tricks, we identify social and cognitive triggers to make our designs stickier and more addictive. So addictive, in fact, that a 2012 study by Wilhelm Hofmann et al. concluded that tweeting or checking emails is harder for people to resist than cigarettes and alcohol.

Good UX designers are said to be emotionally intelligent, good at putting themselves in the shoes of their users. But according to 2013 research done by developmental psychologists Yuki Nozaki and Masuo Koyasu, the dark side of emotional intelligence is that emotionally intelligent people are also very good at manipulating others' behaviors to suit their own interests.

When we design a diet app that celebrates our healthy-eating streaks or create a language-learning app that rewards us with badges, we are using gamification to persuade users to keep going. But when social media apps coerce us to engage by deliberately tapping into our need for quick dopamine and oxytocin hits, or we deliberately wait until a user is fully immersed in game play before we ask for payment, we're taking advantage of them.

So we have a choice. We can either design meaningful, productive experiences that persuade users to achieve their goal, or we can choose to deliberately mislead, deceive, and coerce users for personal gain (see Principle 5).

In our studio, we have had many discussions with our clients where we highlighted some seemingly innocuous yet nefarious or coercive practices. Most of the time, the client was not really aware of it. They just want to hit their targets or KPIs (key performance indicators) and don't really know of any other way to do it. Which is fair; they're not the expert, we are. That's why it's our responsibility to help educate and propose alternatives that don't take advantage of the user.

If all UX designers would think about how every single product or feature they are working on might coerce people into doing something they didn't set out to do and raise the alarm right away, the internet would be a much more positive place.

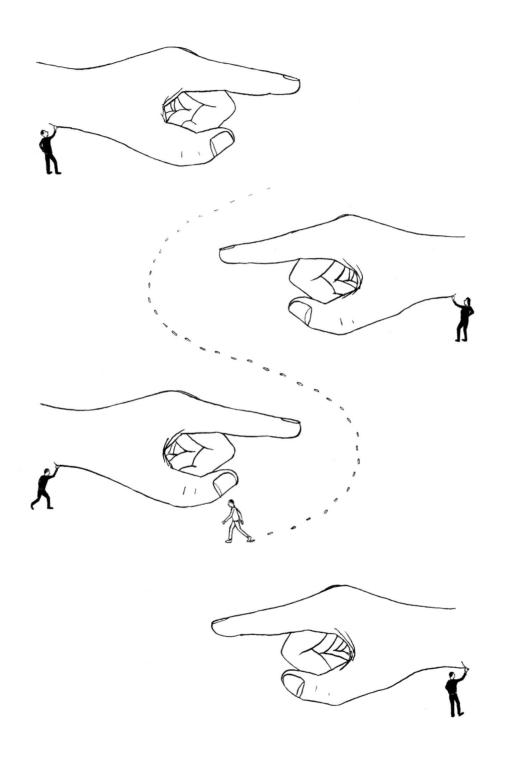

31

Design for passive attention.

Most digital products require interaction to be useful. Twitter, for example, is valuable only if people tweet, like, comment, follow, and keep up with their feed. Otherwise, it's not. This is true for all interfaces, with the exception of smartwatches, activity trackers, or smart home devices like lightbulbs, switches, doorbells, or thermostats. Smart devices don't require any interaction from the user to provide value or be functional.

Smart devices are part of the "Internet of Things," a term coined by Peter T. Lewis in 1985. According to Lewis, the "Internet of Things, or IoT, is the integration of people, processes and technology with connectable devices and sensors to enable remote monitoring, status, manipulation and evaluation of trends of such devices." In other words, any device that is connected to the internet.

When we were working with Google on some clock faces for their Google Nest Hub smart home device, we had a lot of discussions around what the purpose of a screen in the house really is and whether or not a smart home device should even have a display to begin with. Because if it does have a display, it is likely always on, so it should add something to the environment and not feel like one of those TVs that are always on when you walk into a sports bar.

A screen in the house that is always on is not a computer, it's a piece of decoration that is connected to the internet. And decoration is a tricky thing. It's very personal. It's a reflection of who we are and what we like to surround ourselves with. Some people might want to see the album covers of the music they are listening to, while others might prefer a photo slideshow of friends and family. Others might only use it as a way to tell time.

Besides designing a variety of different graphical clock faces that users could choose from, we also scanned Google Earth to find shapes that closely resembled numbers when seen from above, such as a river that looks like the number four, a football stadium that looks like the number zero, and so on. By utilizing Google Earth imagery to design a clock face, we not only took advantage of technology that is unique to Google, but we also ended up with something that wouldn't be possible with a regular analog clock.

Not all interfaces require constant interaction, so thinking about what value a device can bring when it's in idle mode or just ambiently part of the environment is very important. An internet-connected device in the home has unique capabilities that an analog device doesn't. But we have to be very careful with how we use those capabilities and make sure we add to the environment rather than overtake it.

→
Key clock faces we designed for the release of the new Google Nest Hub smart home device. Users were able to choose from a large variety of different clock faces to best match their home decor tastes and preferences.

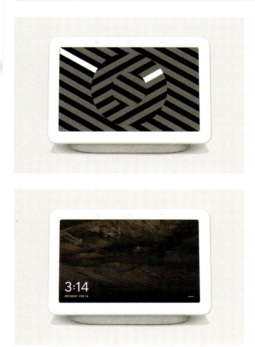

32

Know the purpose.

In the 1970s German industrial designer Dieter Rams said, "Products fulfilling a purpose are like tools. They are neither decorative objects nor works of art. Their design should therefore be both neutral and restrained, to leave room for the user's self-expression."

All digital products are tools and therefore have a purpose. If you're an e-commerce marketplace, people want to buy something; if you're a search engine, people want to search something; and if you're a content platform, people want to read or learn something. When people use a digital product, they have a goal in mind, and they want to be able to achieve that goal as quickly as possible. If they can't, the design has failed.

When we redesigned the website for Markforged, a manufacturer of industrial-grade 3D printers, we knew most users were trying to figure out if they should change from their current subtractive manufacturing process to the additive manufacturing process of 3D printing.

Customers were particularly interested in understanding if the 3D printed materials would be strong enough, if switching to additive manufacturing would speed up the process, and change in cost. After analyzing the existing content, we realized that it required too many clicks to get to this information, and when found, it didn't provide clear enough answers.

Our redesign supported the in-depth content needed to squash these concerns and created an underlying architecture that got users to that information as quickly as possible (see Principle 67).

Regardless of the product, users should be able to quickly and easily complete the task they had in mind. People are not there to admire the design and shouldn't even be thinking about the design. Digital products aren't art galleries—they're tools. They're a means to an end for the user on a mission.

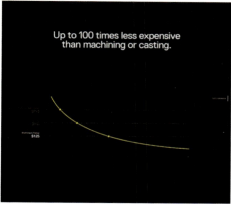

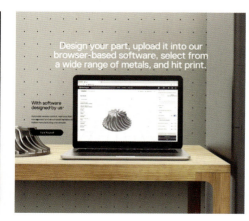

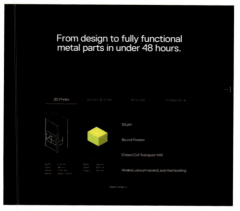

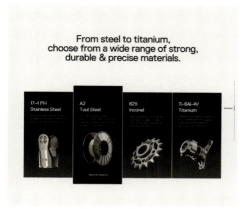

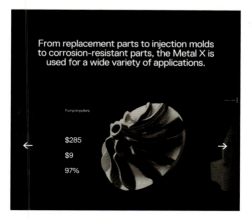

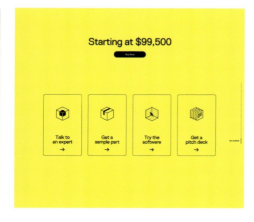

↑
The goal of the Markforged website was to quickly provide relevant and important information about switching to an additive manufacturing process. People could either scan through the key differentiating factors as headlines or deep-dive into details relevant to their specific needs and concerns.

33

Interrupt only when necessary.

Many years ago I decided to turn off all alerts and notifications on all of my devices, with the exception of phone calls and text message alerts from my immediate family. That's because for me to be as productive as possible, I need to be able to completely focus on a task. And I can get into a state of deep concentration only if I'm not constantly being interrupted by unimportant notifications.

On average, according to research by *Harvard Business Review*, we are interrupted every six to twelve minutes by something that actually doesn't require our immediate attention. The *New York Times* app notifies us of breaking news, Twitter tells us we have a new follower, Duolingo reminds us it's time to practice French. My father gets notifications that tell him the front door just opened. He initially had that turned on to alert him of a potential break-in, but since he frequently works from home and people come and go all the time, it drives everybody crazy.

According to research done by Gloria Mark, who studies digital distraction at UC Irvine, it takes an average of twenty-five minutes to return to the original task once we're interrupted. And after that interruption, we don't typically return to the original task right away. We take a break and switch to two other tasks—like quickly replying to emails or checking our social media channels—before returning to whatever it was we were doing before.

Whenever I think about designing for interruptions, I always think back to when I was waiting tables in college. People don't like it when you interrupt them while they're talking, but they also don't like it if you ignore them and they have to flag you down. Good waiters keep an eye on their tables and can be summoned with just a simple head nod or eyebrow raise. Digital interruptions should be the same. They should be relevant, arrive only when needed, and get delivered appropriately (see Principle 34).

Remember, if everything is important, nothing is important. First consider whether the information is even worth interrupting someone for. If the answer is yes, think about how to deliver that message. "YOUR HOUSE IS ON FIRE" versus "YOU JUST RECEIVED AN EMAIL" don't have the same level of importance in the real world. They shouldn't have the same level of importance on our devices either.

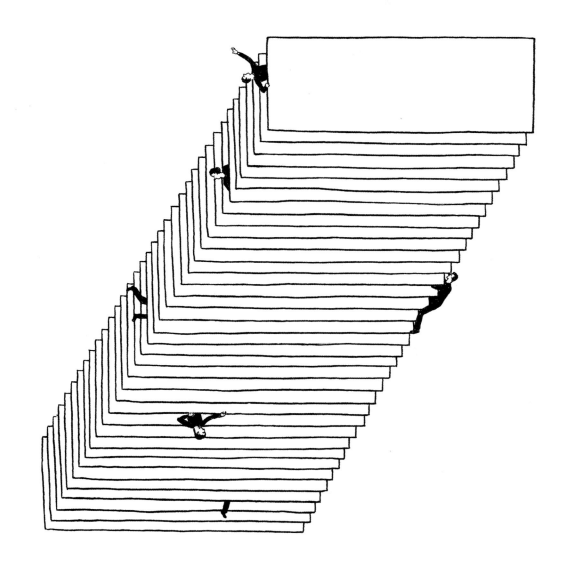

34

Make notifications valuable.

Remember Microsoft's Clippy, the paperclip-shaped assistant spamming us with unhelpful hints and suggestions? Within Microsoft, its internal codename was "TFC," with "C" meaning "clown" and "TF" meaning—well, you can probably guess what that meant. The problem with Clippy—and hints from the system in general—is that when we're in the middle of something, we really hate being interrupted (see Principle 33).

But notifications aren't inherently evil. In fact, oftentimes they can make the overall user experience better. Imagine if there weren't any error messages informing us something was filled out incorrectly, warnings right before we tried to delete something important, or alerts that notified us of important changes. We need notifications.

A valuable notification anticipates moments that might be confusing to the user because it knows what the user is trying to achieve. It also understands the urgency and importance in which the message needs to be conveyed. Before we send a notification, we need to ask ourselves whether we understand what is important to the user in that exact moment or if we are making assumptions on their behalf. That's why it's important to include notifications in our design process early on, not treat them as an afterthought.

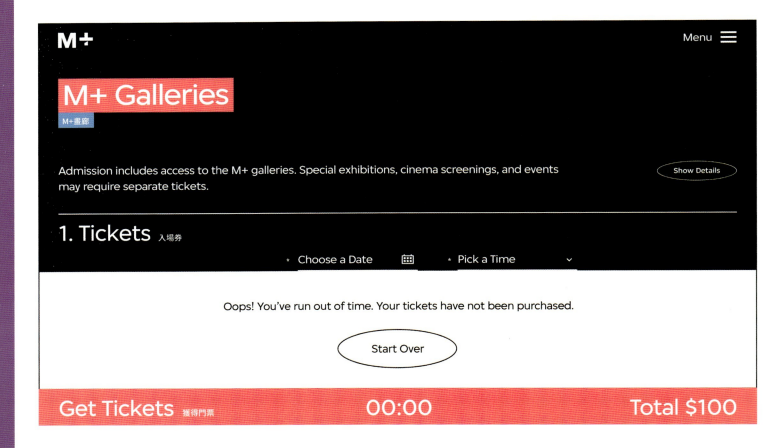

Users don't need to be notified of everything that happens within the system. And since useless alerts are swatted away like flies, we have to be very careful about how many we send. When it comes to notifications, a "less is more" approach is better. If we send too many, people will be conditioned to ignore them, making them miss the ones that actually matter.

As UX designers, we need to master the art of interrupting, otherwise we run the risk of ending up with another Clippy. If we treat the user's time as valuable and think of notifications as an assistant in potential moments of confusion, not as a sales tool, we're on the right track. The guiding principle should always be, "is this actually helpful to the user at this exact moment?" If the answer is no, don't send it.

↓
Examples of important notifications from the M+ museum in Hong Kong that help the user on their way and don't interrupt the user unnecessarily. On the left, the user is notified that they have run out of time to purchase tickets to the museum, and on the right, that the museum is temporarily closed.

35

Minimize form input.

Filling out any type of form is annoying. I don't think any of us have ever been handed a bunch of forms and thought, "Yay, can't wait to fill these out!" Unfortunately, since we can't verbally explain things to a computer (not yet anyway), the only way to buy something, return something, contact a company, or create an account online is to fill out a form. And if we don't enter all the fields or don't do it correctly, we're not allowed to proceed.

Over the course of my career, I have designed many, many, many forms. And on almost every project, I have had to explain to clients that every little field added to a form negatively affects its conversion rate. The more mandatory fields there are, fewer people will complete the entire form. That's why it's very important to make sure we ask only what we really need. Remember that people are doing us a pretty big favor by filling out the form in the first place.

Also clients must consider if they actually need this information. Whenever I ask what they plan on doing with all of this information, the usual response is that there is a grand plan for some sort of magical "customer relationship" database. In the future. At some point. When we get the budget. But the truth is that most of the time all of this data ends up in some black hole that nobody ever looks at again. They're not even doing anything nefarious with it; it's literally just sitting there, waiting to be stolen or hacked.

However, there is a way to make filling out forms fun. The One Shared House 2030 project we did in collaboration with SPACE10 and IKEA about the future of communal living is basically a form disguised as a game. We hid twenty-one questions behind colorless shapes that would reveal the question on click or tap, kind of like an advent calendar. As soon as a question was answered, we'd show the user how their answer stands in relation to everyone else, and the shape would get a color. It was the highest conversion rate we've ever had on any form ever.

Obviously not all forms should feel like a game, but if the form is ordered logically, fields are labeled clearly, related information is grouped, there are proper defaults, both keyboard and thumb input has been considered, autocomplete is provided whenever possible, and we ask only what we really need, more people will complete it (see Principle 11). And when they do, let's make sure there is an actual plan for all of that data.

→
A form that doesn't look like a form, because it's disguised as a game. It's the highest conversion rate we've ever had on any form ever. Over 150,000 people from all over the world completed the form we worked on in collaboration with SPACE10/IKEA that captured and displayed people's preferences around communal living.

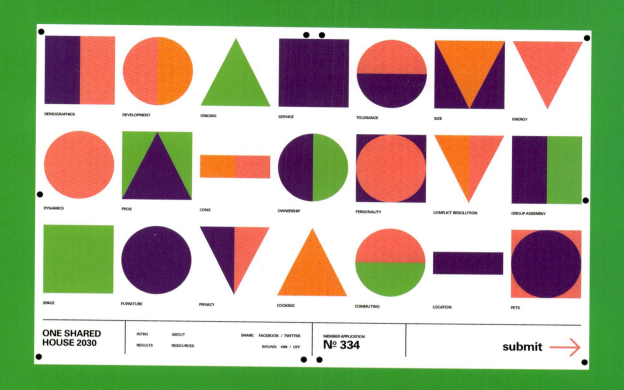

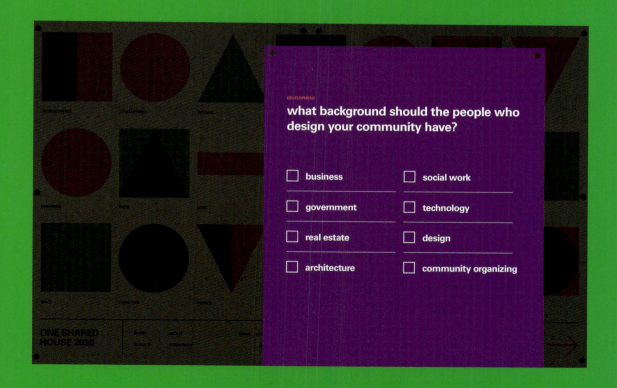

36

Little time,
little design.

Normally when we opt for a minimalist design, we do so because we know it will lower the cognitive load of the user, making the interface easier to interact with (see Principle 11). Or it's for aesthetic purposes. Or to convey a certain feeling or emotion. But sometimes we keep an interface simple because it needs to be designed and built in as little time as possible.

One of the things Anton and I agreed on when we first started our studio is that we would use any kind of downtime between projects for personal experimentation. During these pauses, we create our own project brief and use the available time frame as our deadline to complete whatever we come up with.

The first time we had such a break, we made a mobile game. We thought it would be a good idea to do something with color, as that wouldn't require a lot of design effort and would be easier to complete.

Once we dove into the world of colors, things became interesting. Since each brain responds differently to the stimuli produced when incoming light reacts with the several types of cone cells in the eye, the perception of color is subjective. We also see colors differently depending on gender, ethnicity, geography, and even the language we speak. So we thought it would be interesting to design a game that tests people's perception of color.

We created a simple ten-round game that presented users with a color for three seconds and then asked them to match that color as closely as possible, allowing them to discover the accuracy of their color perception. Since the mechanics of the game were quite simple, it didn't require a whole lot of design or development effort. We were able to concept, design, and launch the entire game within two weeks.

There are many reasons why we might opt for a minimalist design. But since the right solution can oftentimes be found in the simplest of ideas, placing constraints on the design process also helps save time. The fewer elements and features there are, the faster it can be designed and built. And that makes a huge difference when crunched for time.

→
Key screens from our self-initiated ColorMatch iOS game. The inspiration came from an argument we were having about a color. My design partner, Anton, thought it was one color, and I disagreed. To settle the argument, we dug into the science of color perception and created an app that tests how accurate people's color perception actually is.

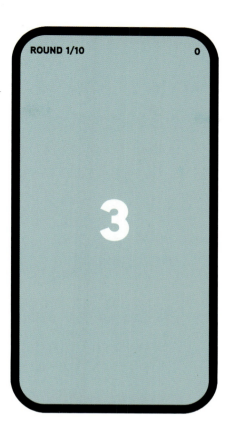

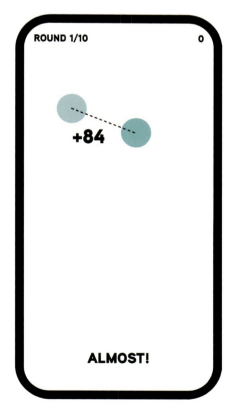

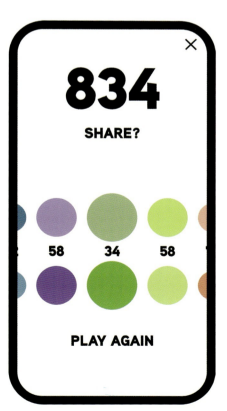

37

Rules are meant to be broken.

High usability is very important when it comes to websites or interfaces where users are trying to complete a task. But if we want to encourage people to play or want to be experimental, making something that violates all usability rules and is deliberately anti user friendly can actually increase engagement (see Principle 29).

But before we start breaking the internet, it's important to at least be aware of the norm. In 1990, Jakob Nielson one of the world's foremost experts in web usability, developed a list of ten heuristics for user interface design. This list has become the gold standard for usability ever since:

1. Keep users informed about what is going on through appropriate feedback within a reasonable amount of time.
2. Follow real-world conventions, make information appear in a natural and logical order, and use words, phrases, and concepts familiar to the user.
3. Provide a clear exit to leave unwanted actions.
4. Follow platform and industry conventions so users don't have to wonder whether different words, situations, or actions mean the same thing.
5. Eliminate error-prone conditions, or present users with a confirmation option before they commit to the action.
6. Minimize the user's memory load, and make sure information required to use the design is visible or easily retrievable when needed.
7. Cater to both inexperienced and experienced users.
8. Remove irrelevant or rarely needed information.
9. Express error messages in plain language, precisely indicate the problem, and constructively suggest a solution.
10. Provide documentation to help users understand how to complete their tasks.

On the homepage of the British artist Shantell Martin, we have a hidden feature—a little Easter egg—that deliberately breaks all of these rules. If users are able to find the word "Play," an interactive panel appears that wreaks havoc on all of Shantell's drawings, making the interface almost unusable. Most people didn't find it, but those who did ended up spending enormous amounts of time playing around with it.

Usability shouldn't always be the main consideration. If we don't need people to perform a specific task and just want to encourage them to play, high usability can actually stifle exploration. That's why the most popular games are also the hardest to figure out. Kids also love apps and websites that actually score very low in usability. Why? Because interfaces that score low in usability keep their parents out.

→
The hidden Easter egg on Shantell Martin's homepage allows people to decide if they would like Shantell's artwork to Dance, Party, or Love. Once selected, users can play with the slider to determine how much of the artwork is affected, and how fast, chaotic, and strong the reaction should be.

We have to ask
questions, read
lines, follow the
and be good d

he right
oetween the
ight hunches,
tectives.

38

Choose the right client.

There is not a single scenario in which it's worth dealing with a bad client. Let me say that again. There is not a single scenario in which it's worth dealing with a bad client. You're better off eating ramen noodles for a month than dealing with a client who demands you start designing before you understand the problem, wants you to work out of order, tries to do your work for you, blocks access to their people, takes forever to make a decision, ignores project goals in favor of organizational politics, or doesn't respect your design process. Trust me, it's not worth it.

When Alexander Wang was creative director at Balenciaga, they came over to our office to discuss a potential collaboration, and I said to him that we want to ensure working together will be more like dating because we're not prostitutes. Our account manager gasped and kicked me under the table. Luckily the entire Balenciaga team burst out laughing. But it's true. Depending on the size of the project, you're going to have to work together anywhere from three months to a year. That's a relationship. And that's a long time to deal with any red flags you chose to ignore when you agreed to do the work.

Even if your favorite brand or product in the world calls, pay very close attention to how they behave from the very first moment of contact, as that will be indicative of how they'll behave throughout the project. Do they take forever to answer emails? Are they hard to pin down? Are they overly concerned with fees and money? Do they understand and respect the process of UX? Is this project important to them, or is it something they don't really care about? Are they open to new ideas? Are they open to change? Are they innovative themselves? Do you *like* them?

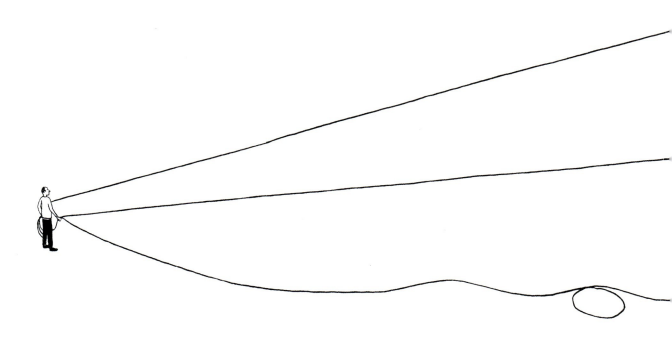

I have learned the hard way that if my gut tells me something is a little fishy in the early stages of business development—even if I can't quite put my finger on it— the project will be a disaster. And if a bad client does manage to slip through our evaluation process or they reveal themselves as such later on, the only thing we can do is learn from the experience. What is it that made them bad? Why did this problem arise in the first place? What could we have done to prevent it? What lessons have we learned that we can apply in the future?

Tolstoy's 1877 novel *Anna Karenina* starts with this sentence: "All happy families are alike; each unhappy family is unhappy in its own way." And the same is true for client relationships. Positive client relationships share a common set of attributes that lead to a great project, while a variety of attributes can lead to a bad client relationship. That's why it's important to make a conscious effort to screen for bad clients prior to signing any contracts, because there is not a single scenario in which it's worth dealing with a bad client.

39

Be a good detective.

Before we start any work, I always tell our clients that we are not—and will never be—the expert on their business. But we are the experts on moving them through a design process that will benefit their customers, which in turn will help their business. But to do that, we first need to dig into what the client is trying to achieve.

Some clients, especially if they have a dedicated digital team, have already done a ton of research, are super organized, are clear on what they need, and have put all of that thinking in writing. Other clients may not have prepared as extensively and only have a top-level hunch that they need us to validate (see Principle 56). Either way, we still have to get up to speed before we kick off design production with these two activities:

Initial questions
To be as prepared as possible for the kickoff meeting, we first send over some questions. We ask about the roles of the project members, what they can tell us about their target audience, what they think about their competitors, where they think they need to do better, how they're currently handling making updates, what they would love to have if time and money weren't issues, and who will ultimately be responsible for signing off on our work.

Kickoff meeting
Once we have digested that, we set up a four-hour meeting (ideally in person) with their core project team to go through our questions, clarify requirements, review existing design documentation, understand their current workflows, identify what they know about their customer needs, and brainstorm how we could potentially help their users achieve their goals.

Afterwards, we put together a document with everything we have learned with one clear problem statement that this project will need to address. This is our North Star. Every decision will have to map to that. If we don't agree on this up front, or we don't figure out early on where there could potentially be pushback or delay, that negative domino effect will be felt at every single decision point later on.

I always tell my students that besides being good at design, a good UX designer also has to be a good detective and a good therapist. We have to be able to make people feel comfortable, ask the right questions, read between the lines, and follow the right hunches. These soft skills are extremely important for the design process to go as smoothly as possible, and they help ensure we end up with a design that solves the right problem.

40

Gather requirements.

Besides reading through any existing documentation (see Principle 56), we start each project by interviewing business stakeholders and potential end-users. During these interviews, which are about thirty minutes each, we ask open-ended questions to encourage interviewees to share their thoughts in greater detail.

These semistructured, qualitative interviews are a tool borrowed from social sciences, and they're designed to be open enough so topics can be explored that we wouldn't have been able to imagine beforehand. Our client contact helps figure out who to talk to within their organization, and together we select from their current customers. The goal is to obtain knowledge from the business stakeholders while better understanding how the end-user might be experiencing the product.

We try to talk to fifteen to twenty business stakeholders across as many departments as possible, and we share what we'd like to cover beforehand. During the interview, we take handwritten notes (people tend to be less candid if they know they are being recorded) and ask open-ended questions like "What have you already tried?," "why is this project important now?," and "How will this change be perceived from inside the company?"

Once the business stakeholder interviews are done, we interview about fifteen current customers, asking questions like "What has your experience been like with this product so far?," "Do you remember a time where you were frustrated?," or "Talk me through how you approach this task."

After our interviews, we compile a document that summarizes our key findings. We highlight any assumptions we heard, requirements that were brought up, or prescriptive solutions that were offered. We then discuss with the core project team which insights we want to consider and which comments to ignore.

The product definition—or understanding—phase sets the foundation for the final product. Only after we understand what actually matters to the business stakeholders and customers can we start thinking of ways to conduct the research. And only after we have done the research can we actually start designing.

Define

41

Define the problem statement.

Every time we work on self-initiated projects in our studio—projects that are for ourselves and not for a client—we create our own brief, set our own deadlines, and determine the problem statement ourselves. That's because design is not art and needs to solve a real human need. As the American minimalist artist Donald Judd famously said, "Design has to work, art does not." And we cannot make the design work without defining the problem first.

Whenever we're facing an open brief, it helps to add some artificial constraints and self-enforce a few rules. Constraints enable us to narrow potential solutions and allow for ideas that wouldn't be possible without them. An endless scope of possibilities can be quite paralyzing when trying to come up with an idea.

At the same time, the brief can't be too limiting—there still has to be enough space to allow for surprising solutions. When I was doing my master's in communications design at Pratt, a professor once said to me that if the brief is "design a better toothbrush," you will always end up with something that looks like a toothbrush. But if you open up the problem statement to "design a better way to clean your mouth," the solution might not look like a toothbrush at all and might even be better than a toothbrush.

When we were working on our interactive documentary *One Shared House*, our artificial constraint was time—the story had to be told in ten minutes or less—and since we wanted people to watch the video (which makes people lean back), while also interacting with the background information (which makes people lean in), our problem statement became "make switching between watching the video and reading the background information feel natural."

Being very literal about the project's goal helps kick-start the ideation process and creates a solid framework to measure all future decisions against. Without restraints or a good problem statement, it's hard to know where to even start, which can feel overwhelming and paralyze the design process. If we have a clear framework, it's easier for people to stay on track, and we are more likely to solve the right problem in a surprising way.

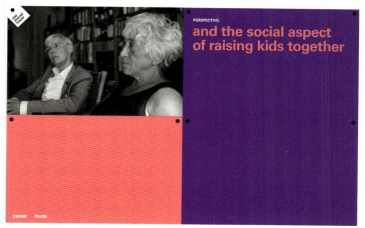

PERSPECTIVE:

and the social aspect of raising kids together

pause   mute

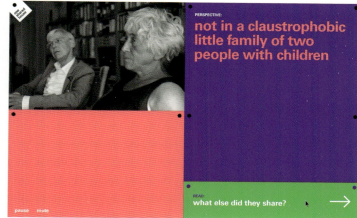

PERSPECTIVE:

not in a claustrophobic little family of two people with children

pause   mute

READ:
what else did they share?   →

daily house dinner

official 8-page rental contract, 1984

✕

what else did they share?

- ● Kitchen
- ● Garden
- ● Washing Machine
- ● Bathrooms

- ● Rooftop
- ● House Meetings
- ● Daily Dinners
- ● Communal / TV Room

They settled into their rooms, started having communal dinners and hanging out in the communal room, kitchen, and garden. The adults built a darkroom, a crafts corner, a guest room, and a painting studio.

They met up with groups from other communal homes, threw parties, hosted dinners, and got involved in city politics. They were hailed in the press as a shining example of communal living at its best.

↑
Key screens from our self-produced interactive documentary *One Shared House* about my experience growing up in a communal house in the center of Amsterdam. Since our problem statement was "make switching between watching the video and reading the background information feel natural," we looked at early video games that combined storytelling with interactions, like *Where in the World Is Carmen Sandiego?* and *The Legend of Zelda.*

42

Find shortcuts.

Some projects have a loosely defined launch date determined by the features that will be included, whereas others have a very fixed deadline that must be hit, no matter what. If a project does have a strict deadline, any proposals from the concepting phase need to be able to be executed within the agreed upon time. So we have to be very careful with what we propose (see Principle 44).

When working with the History Channel on a digital feature about the 150th anniversary of the American Civil War, we agreed to do six interactive infographics that would be interesting for both Civil War fanatics and seventh graders learning about it for the first time. Since an anniversary happens on a specific day, we knew there would be no wiggle room when it came to the deadline.

During our requirements gathering at the start of the project (see Principle 40), the core client team told us that whenever they would do any feature on the Civil War, hardcore fans—you know, the type that dress up and reenact battles on the weekend—would send complaints about any spotted historical inaccuracies. People would get so worked up over things like the color of the buttons on a Confederate soldier's uniform being wrong, they would send literal hate mail.

Since we were planning to illustrate these infographics, they told us that whatever illustrations we came up with needed to be historically accurate. Historically accurate?! We literally had two weeks slated for design research, and there was no way in hell we would be able to research whether the illustrations would be historically accurate or not.

Back at the studio, we discussed it with the team, and after some brainstorming, we stumbled upon a genius shortcut. We decided that the entire experience would happen at night so people would only ever see the silhouettes of the soldiers, without any details that could be pulled apart for their historical inaccuracies. When we presented it to the History Channel and told them about our time-saving cheat, they all burst out laughing. We agreed on the design direction that day and continued on with production as planned.

Going through a thorough requirements-gathering process allows us to unearth the underwater stones, roadblocks, or potential time sucks. Had we not spent as much time talking to the History Channel upfront, we probably would have ended up wasting a lot of time on a design direction that would have gotten rejected right away. All projects come with some sort of limitation, and it's important to know what they are up front so we can find the right shortcuts to speed up the process without sacrificing quality.

CIVIL**WAR**150

COMMEMORATING THE 150TH ANNIVERSARY OF **THE AMERICAN CIVIL WAR**

WHO THEY
WERE

WEAPONS
OF WAR

HOW THEY
DIED

EXPLORE
and
VOTE

5 DEADLIEST
BATTLES

PAYING
FOR THE WAR

WEST POINT
WARRIORS

Make Some Noise

MOST POPULAR TOPICS
as voted by our viewers

Robert E. Lee	Abraham Lincoln	George W. Washington	Ulysses S. Grant	Thomas Jefferson	Stonewall Jackson
653 votes	**354 votes**	**154 votes**	**653 votes**	**653 votes**	**653 votes**

What were the
HISTORIAN'S PICKS?

We asked a panel of historians to
select the essential topics that defined
the American Civil War.

View Their **Picks**

SHARE CIVIL**WAR**150

↑
The History Channel site for the 150th anniversary of the
American Civil War happens at night and only shows soldiers
in silhouettes. This creative direction saved an enormous
amount of design research time and simultaneously
minimized the potential for historical inaccuracies.

43

Done is better than perfect.

Every single thing on a website or app that a user can interact with is considered a feature. Filtering, sorting, pagination, image carousels, booking tickets, or selecting seats are all features. One of the hardest things on any project is figuring out which features are must-haves and which are nice to have, but not crucial.

To get a product out as quickly as possible, it's best to release products with the bare minimum amount of features required to see how people will interact with it. Otherwise we run the risk of taking forever to release a very large, bloated, and expensive product nobody wants or needs (see Principle 44).

The term "minimum viable product" (MVP) was first coined by Frank Robinson in 2001 and is a development technique in which a product is released with only the core features required for deployment. Must-have features are included in the first release, and nice-to-have features are identified but planned for a later release. So if we're designing a plane, for example, the MVP would contain only the features that actually make the plane fly. The carpet, passenger seats, toilets, or overhead compartments would be slated for a later release.

In our studio, to get to an MVP, we have what is basically a glorified spreadsheet that describes and imagines all the potential features in writing before we decide to design or build any of them. We solicit input from the business stakeholders and add the features that directly relate to a business objective. Then we add the features that map to the users' needs.

Once all features are clearly described, unambiguous, and concise, we measure each feature based on its business value, user value, and technical complexity on a scale of high/medium/low.

After this exercise, we can clearly see which features are our must-haves (features with high business value, high user value, and low technical complexity) and nice-to-haves (features with low business value, low user value, and high technical complexity). We then regroup with the project team and decide what will make it into our MVP versus a later release.

Planning features early on in the project life cycle is vital because it allows us to define the product strategy and the road to achieve it from the start. It also creates greater cohesion within our team and with the client by managing scope, and it gets the product to users as soon as possible.

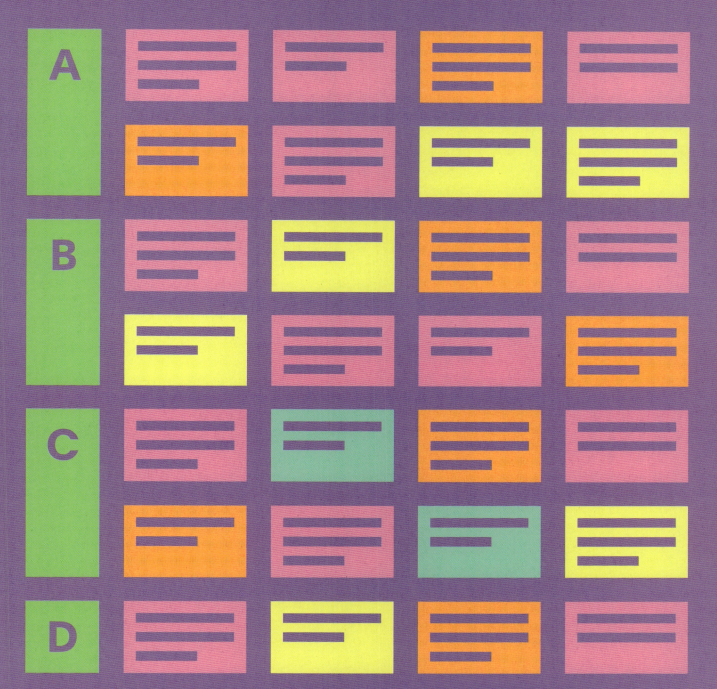

44

Underpromise and overdeliver.

Understanding which features to include from a business perspective is quite easy, as that requires conversations with only the business stakeholders. But figuring out which features should be included for the users is a little trickier. It's not as simple as only including the bare necessities for the launch (see Principle 43). It's also important to include some features that the user isn't expecting and will be positively surprised by.

So how do we decide which additional features to include in the MVP? You may have a hunch, but it's good to have a more systematic approach to feature prioritization, especially if you have to justify decisions to business stakeholders. Prior to determining whether a feature has a high, medium, or low user value, it's good to ask these questions first:

- Does the user expect the feature to be there?
- Does the user not care about this feature either way?
- Does this feature have the potential to actively upset the user?
- Does this feature positively surprise the user?
- Does this feature allow users to optimize the use of the interface?

This method of feature prioritization is loosely based on a model created in 1984 by Noriaki Kano, a professor of quality management at the Tokyo University of Science, who developed this framework while researching the factors that contribute to customer satisfaction and loyalty. Though not specifically created for designing interfaces, it's a very handy way to quickly understand which features should make it into the final product.

When we were working on the members directory of the Art Directors Guild (a labor union representing film and television professionals), we needed to design an easier way for members of the art department to get hired. We created public profiles where members could list their skills and credits, along with contact information. From an MVP perspective, that would have been sufficient. However, since we had everyone's credits stored in the database, we decided to cross-reference which members worked on which productions together, making it easier for members to find entire teams for a production. Nobody asked for that feature, yet when we launched, it was the one feature members were most excited about.

It's important to keep in mind that features that delight users now could become expected features later on. For example, the crowd may have gasped when Steve Jobs introduced the pinch-to-zoom functionality in the first iPhone at the 2007 Apple event, but we're not gasping now. As technology evolves, we become more and more demanding in the types of features we expect. That's why it's important to continuously re-evaluate the interface and release new features every once in a while that have the potential to wow users once again.

→
Members of the Art Directors Guild can quickly see all the members of the guild who worked on the same production, making it easier to find entire production teams who've worked together before.

THE UNICORN
SEASON 1 & 2
ART DIRECTOR
👤 3

EMERGENCE
PILOT
SUPERVISING ART DIRECTOR
👤 1

THE FIX
SEASON 1
ART DIRECTOR

MARVEL'S RUNAWAYS
SEASON 1
ART DIRECTOR
👤 14

MORE PRODUCTION MEMBERS

 YVONNE BOUDREAUX
SET DESIGNER

 BRETT MCKENZIE
ART DIRECTOR

 KEDRA DAWKINS
ASSISTANT ART DIRECTOR

 DARCY PREVOST
SET DESIGNER

 BRADLEY ARNOLD
STORYBOARD ARTIST

EL CAMINO CHRISTMAS
ART DIRECTOR
👤 3

POWERLESS
SEASON 1
ART DIRECTOR
👤 3

ART DIRECTOR
👤 12

WHITNEY
ART DIRECTOR
👤 1

REAL HUSBANDS OF HOLLYWOOD
SEASON 3
ART DIRECTOR
👤 5

EPISODES
LA UNIT - SEASON 4
ART DIRECTOR
👤 1

SURVIVING JACK
PILOT, SEASON 1
ART DIRECTOR
👤 1

RED STATE
ART DIRECTOR

JOIN
DIRECTORY
AVAILABI...
EVENTS
AWARDS
THE GUILD
STORE

👤 MEMBER...

SEARCH

45

Introduce complexity only when necessary.

The biggest discussions in any project are always about the feature set—what will users actually be able to do in the final product? Most of the time, stakeholders get stuck on a cool idea without asking if it's essential in helping the user achieve their goal. Our job as UX designers is to advocate for the user's needs, ruthlessly editing down unnecessary content and functionality that will get in their way (see Principle 11).

In our studio, we always start with the simplest solution and introduce complexity only when necessary, not just for the user's sake but also for our own sanity. We have to get the project done on time and within budget, and whatever we design needs to be easy to build and maintain as well.

To cut through complexity and guide our decision-making process, we follow a commonly used guiding principle: Occam's razor, which comes from the fourteenth-century English scholastic philosopher and theologian William of Ockham. He wrote: "*Numquam ponenda est pluralitas sine necessitate*," or "Plurality must never be posited without necessity." The razor refers to shaving away anything that isn't necessary.

When working on the new website for the Art Directors Guild, we were inundated with feature requests from various committee members. Many of these requests would have made the product a complicated mess, and we knew that was not going to benefit their members or the project's timeline.

After many meetings that ended in gridlock, we walked into the executive director's office—who had commissioned the work—to ask how we should explain to the committee members that we cannot possibly add all the features they want. He looked up, and with a smirk he said, "Tell them people in hell want ice water."

Occam's razor is not an example of simplicity for simplicity's sake. It is used to cut through the clutter to find the best solution based on the knowledge at hand, without compromising the overall function. By shaving away complexity, features will have more clarity and impact, allowing people to use the product more efficiently.

→
The homepage for the Art Directors Guild, a labor union representing film and television professionals, is a scrollable website that has only relevant features and content that update most frequently. More complicated features were moved to other parts of the experience.

JOIN
DIRECTORY
EVENTS
AWARDS
THE GUILD

MEMBER LOG IN

SEARCH

SCENIC ART: PAINTING THROUGH TIME

→

← →

SAMUEL MICHLAP
SENIOR ILLUSTRATOR

→

ALL MEMBERS

DANIELA V MEDEIROS
JUNIOR SET DESIGNER / ART DIRECTOR · FILM / ART DIRECTOR · COMMERCIALS

→

18 JUL MODEL: YUKO HOUSTON →
FIGURE DRAWINGS WORKSHOP. 7PM · 10PM / ADG, ROBERT BOYLE STUDIO 800

22 AUG TRIBUTE TO JAROSLAV GEBR →
GALLERY 800. RUNS THROUGH JULY 27 / GALLERY 800

6 SEP THE CABINET OF DR. CALIGARI →
FILM SOCIETY. 7PM · 10PM / ADG, ROBERT BOYLE STUDIO 800

30 OCT COMIC-CON 2018: PREVIEW NIGHT →
COMIC-CON. 1:30PM · 2:30PM / SAN DIEGO CONVENTION CENTER

ALL EVENTS

ART DIRECTORS
Develop the overall look of the story, and collaborate with and supervise other departments in managing the creation of physical and digital set elements.

---

design graphics for the camera set and print advertising; create main titles and screen advertising for film and television.

→

SCENIC, TITLE & GRAPHIC ARTISTS
Develop designs for sets and scenery, by hand or using computer software to draft construction drawings and build set models.

→

JACKIE'S DESIGN. CREATING THE WHITE HOUSE IN PARIS.
PERSPECTIVE MAGAZINE

ALL ARTICLES

→

FOLLOW ADG
FACEBOOK
TWITTER
INSTAGRAM

CONTACT
ADG ARCHIVES
MEDIA

AVAILABILITY LIST
PERSPECTIVE
PRESS

INSTAGRAM
FACEBOOK
TWITTER

PRIVACY POLICY
TERMS OF USE
THE IATSE

ART DIRECTORS GUILD
11969 VENTURA BLVD
STUDIO CITY, CA 91604
(818) 762-9995

IATSE LOCAL 800 / © 2018 ART DIRECTORS GUILD

46

Some complexity cannot be reduced.

I'm writing this book on a 2020 MacBook Air. It's the thinnest and lightest computer I've ever had and quite possibly the most beautiful one as well. But I curse it on an almost daily basis. There's not a single USB, HDMI, or SD card input, which means that every time I need to connect to a screen, move files, or access my external hard drive, I need to first connect to a very expensive dongle that was not included with the laptop. By making the product thinner, lighter, and simpler, Apple has made my life more complicated.

This is in direct violation of Tesler's law, which argues that for any system, there is a certain level of complexity that cannot be reduced. The law was coined by computer scientist Larry Tesler in the mid-1980s while he was working for Xerox PARC, and states that complexity does not disappear, but simply moves from one area to another. In other words, complexity is like a balloon. If we squeeze it on the user's end, it will inflate on the development side, and if we squeeze it on the development side, it will inflate on the user's end.

With literally thousands of product SKUs and variations to choose from, the most complicated product portfolio we have ever worked on was for Austrian lighting company Zumtobel. Finding the right information density for the sophisticated target audience of lighting designers and architects was incredibly hard, and we spent a lot of time thinking through the structure of the data. How dense is too dense? How dense is dense enough?

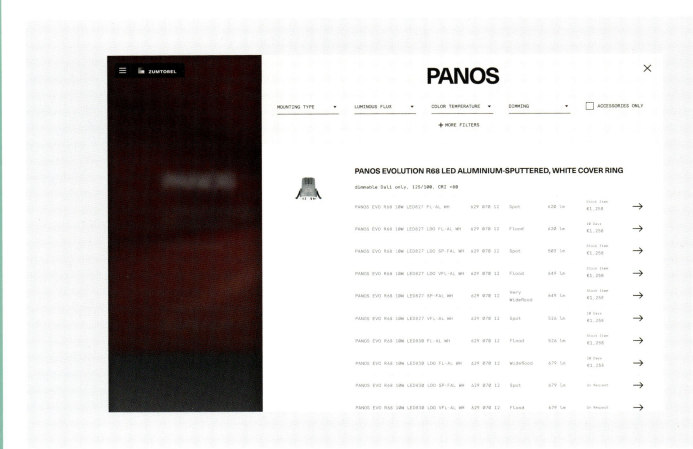

Before we got started, our initial gut instinct was to remove as much complexity from the interface as possible, but after speaking to actual customers, we learned that some level of complexity needs to remain, because a certain level of control is not only needed but expected.

Rather than worrying about simplifying the number of lighting parameters users could choose from in the product portfolio on the interface and moving that complexity to the product database, we decided to keep the complexity on the user's side, creating a robust filtering system with lots of detailed parameters.

Simple actions require simple tools, but complex actions require complex tools. Rather than trying to actually simplify complex functionality, we need to make it *feel* simpler.

The amount of information on Zumtobel's website might seem overwhelming to the layman's eye, but the sophisticated audience of lighting designers and architects required a high level of control and expected to be able to see all relevant information before making a decision on a lighting fixture or solution. The high level of information density was designed on purpose.
↓

47

Imagine the user journey.

When talking about a user's goal—for example, ordering a car service—it can be hard to imagine what a user actually experiences to achieve that goal. On the surface, it sounds pretty straightforward. We connect a rider with a driver, and the user is able to get to where they're going. The end. But if we look closely, it's actually a lot more complicated than that.

Users bring certain expectations, and to meet or even surpass those expectations, it's important to break down each instance where the user interacts with the product and imagine worst-case scenarios. In the world of UX, this is called the user journey, and doing so will ground your decisions in reality—and not wishful thinking—and will allow you to come up with ways to identify and mitigate problems ahead of time.

Let's imagine a user who frequently switches between different apps to get to the cheapest car service option. What might the user do to ensure they're getting the cheapest rate? What would make them feel comfortable deciding? What if they've decided but there aren't any drivers available? What if the driver arrives late? What if the driver takes an unplanned detour, or drives dangerously, or is rude? What if the user left something in the car, or wants to leave a bad rating but feels bad doing so?

Mapping out the entire user journey not only helps us get ahead of issues that might arise, but it also allows business stakeholders—who might be looking only at KPIs (key performance indicators) through a dehumanizing spreadsheet—gain empathy for the user. It also identifies where there's room for improvement and who owns that improvement. Is it something that can be solved with design alone? Or is it a structural change that needs to be solved on the business side as well?

If we don't assume worst-case scenarios when thinking about the user's journey, we run the risk of accidentally ending up with an idealized narrative that doesn't reflect reality, which could make us miss out on the very real opportunities to turn an OK experience into an amazing one (see Principle 41).

48

Create a user flow.

At the beginning of each school year, many of my students (who are doing a master's in interaction design) don't really understand the difference between a user journey and a user flow. It's not their fault really; these terms are very similar, and unless you work in UX, it's hard to understand the difference based on their names alone.

So here's how they differ. When mapping out the user journey, we are considering all of the product's touchpoints. (If we keep with the car service analogy, that would include thinking about using a car service app, actually ordering a car, being in the car, being dropped off, and even interacting with customer service (see Principle 47). A user flow, however, describes only the user's experience inside the app itself, not the entire ecosystem of the product outside of the app.

User flows are usually represented by a diagram that shows the actions the user has to take inside the interface to accomplish their goal. Each action is represented by a rectangle and each decision point by a diamond, and they are connected by arrows representing the direction the user has to take.

Besides showing the happy path, which is the quickest path to success, a user flow also maps out all possible alternative paths to understand where there might be unnecessary friction. And once that friction has been identified, we can optimize and streamline that specific path for the user.

The great thing about user flows is that with very little effort, before we even design any UI or do any information architecture, we can get a bird's-eye view of all the possible paths available to the user. The other nice thing is that as a deliverable, they're quite easy to understand. Everyone—including clients and developers—can understand rectangles connected by arrows.

Unfortunately, whenever we discuss user flows in class, my students' eyes glaze over. The vast majority of them would much rather be working on the layout of a screen than on this abstract schematic. If I had a nickel for each time I heard a student say "I HATE USER FLOWS," I would have been able to retire by now. But here's the good news: There's no wrong or right way of doing them. As long as they're understandable to everyone on the project and weird moments of friction are discovered, you're doing it right.

It's nearly impossible to design the most efficient path to a user's goal right from the start. That's why it's important to try various approaches to ensure that the overall user experience is based on a solid framework. The path the user has to take to reach their goal takes priority over the more visual aspects of the job like UI design or information architecture.

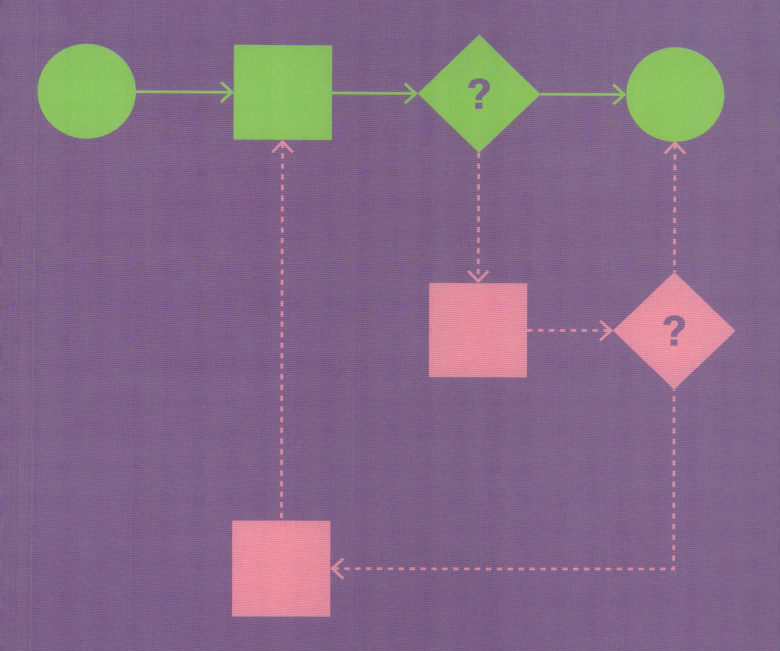

49

Remove barriers and obstacles.

Let's dive into some concrete ways of *how* to remove unnecessary friction, barriers, and obstacles from the user's path. A good user flow maps out one goal at a time, always has a clear starting point and end goal as its title, and only looks at ways to shorten the path between those two specific points (see Principle 48). (Like, for example, from ordering a car to rating the driver.)

Since we read from left to right, the happy path (what we want users to do) should always read in our natural reading direction, and the alternative paths (what users could also possibly do) should always fork upward or downward. That way it's easy to see at a glance how fast or slow the happy path already is and how simple or complicated all the alternative paths are.

It's also important to make sure each action is clearly labeled and to the point, void of jargon or overly wordy labels that contain unnecessary information. Doing so will not only help ensure that all audiences can understand what has been mapped out, it also allows the UX designer to easily return to a previously closed or paused project without skipping a beat.

Now, as far as visualizing everything, any shape or color works, as long as they're clearly marked in the legend and applied consistently. In our studio, we use the following conventions:

Circles for entry and exit points
Transition arrows for user navigation
Green outline for the happy path
Red outline for the alternative path
Rectangles for notes
Diamonds for decisions

Once the entire flow has been mapped out, it's time to review each action or decision point and identify unnecessary moments of friction. Are there ways you can get to the end of the flow in a faster or simpler way? If the answer is yes, and you've discovered some steps that could be optimized or removed, it's time to update the user flow with the newly shortened path. And then it's time to review it again. And again. And again. And so on and so forth, until there is nothing left to remove and you're left with the most optimal way to go from point A to point B.

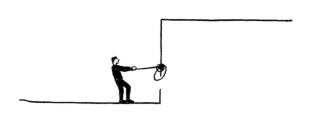

50

What isn't there matters.

Across all creative fields, what *isn't* there is just as important as what *is* there. In fashion, Coco Chanel advised, "Before you leave the house, look in the mirror and take one thing off." In music, Miles Davis famously quipped, "It's not the notes you play, it's the notes you don't play." In design, Jan Tschichold noted that "white space is to be regarded as an active element, not a passive background.

The same holds true when designing interfaces. Except that in the world of UX, the gaps or spaces are about the way features and content are presented to the user during a specific interaction. Or rather, how they're *not* presented to the user. It could mean hiding the navigation when the user is actively reading, collapsing information that isn't relevant to the current task, or breaking up content into digestible little chunks so they contain only the bare minimum number of words required to get the point across (see Principle 11).

When users are left with only the features and content they really need and nothing else, usability and scannability immediately improves, structure and navigation is understood much faster, goals and tasks are achieved much quicker, and fewer mistakes are made overall. On top of that, bounce rates are reduced, retention rates go up, and people tend to feel that the site or app is more credible.

However, we can't simply hide features and call it a day. In fact, we have to be very careful if we do decide to suppress items and be sure to choose the right method and visual indicators to not confuse users. So before we decide to suppress certain features, we need to ask ourselves the following questions first:

1. Do we truly understand the user's intent in this exact interaction?
2. Are we hiding things that stop the user from progressing?
3. Are there clear indicators that point to what's hidden?
4. Is it easy to recall the hidden features?
5. Have we tested the interaction to ensure it works as we imagined?

At times, not showing features can hold just as much value as showing them. By suppressing features people don't need, we help highlight the ones they do. We just need to make sure that whenever we do decide to hide less-used features, there are easy-to-understand trigger indicators, and we don't inadvertently make the interface harder to use.

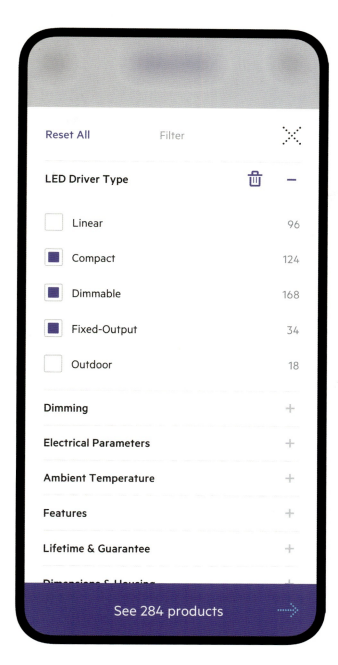

↑
The everyday example of this principle is how things like filters are suppressed by default, only appearing when the user needs them. Shown are two different mobile states for the Austrian lighting components manufacturer Tridonic (sister company of Zumtobel). The default state is on the left, and the filtered view is on the right.

51

Pointing devices inform functionality.

Pointing devices in the field of HCI (human-computer interaction) refer to any kind of input that allows the user to control an interface. For desktop computers, that's commonly the mouse. For laptops, it's the touchpad, and for smartphones and tablets, it's our finger. But there are many more kinds of pointing devices. A stylus, joystick, trackball, or Wii remote are also types of pointing devices. There are even special glasses that allow us to control computers with our eyes.

In 1954, long before the personal computer revolution of the 1970s, American psychologist Paul Fitts developed a mathematical model of human motion that states that the further the distance and the smaller the target's size, the longer it takes for a person to hit the target physically. He proved that this was true across all demographics, regardless of what limb was used (he even tested lips and feet!) and in every condition (even underwater!).

This work was first referenced in HCI in a study by computer research scientist Stuart Card that compared the performance of different pointing devices. The study showed that the mouse beat out all others in terms of speed and accuracy, resulting in Xerox's introduction of the mouse for their Alto computer in 1973.

Today, Fitts's law is often referenced in UX when determining the speed and efficiency of an interface to ensure we don't slow down the user unnecessarily. Since small objects that are spread apart take the longest time to select, the easiest way to ensure efficiency in any interface—regardless of the pointing device—is to make all interactive items as large as possible, place items in sequence close to each other, and provide enough space between items.

If, for example, a user is creating a new calendar event on one side of the screen, we don't want them to have to move their mouse all the way to the other side of the screen to hit the confirm button. Or if the user is holding their mobile device in their right hand, we don't want to force them to move their thumb all the way to the top right of the screen to send a message they are writing on the bottom of the screen.

Meaningful actions should consume meaningful space. Before we try to figure out where to place interactive elements, we first need to consider the context of use and determine which pointing devices are applicable (see Principle 84). That way we can ensure the interface will be as efficient as possible and actually map to the user's goals and reality.

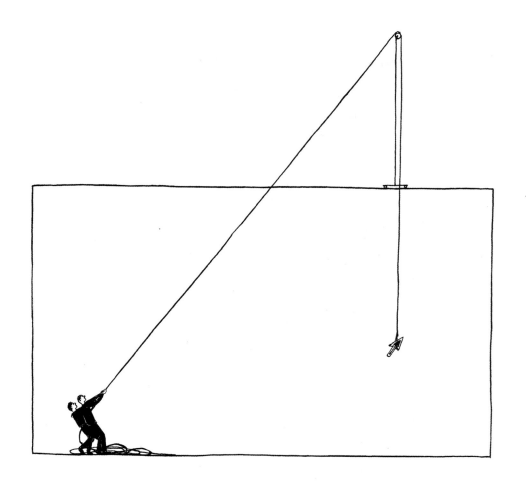

Most compani
design researc
a pseudo-scie

s selling
are selling
ific con.

52

Design cannot be fully objective.

In 1972, in the annex of the Stedelijk Museum in Amsterdam, Dutch graphic designers Wim Crouwel and Jan van Toorn debated whether objectivity or subjectivity works better in design. Crouwel argued in favor of the graphic designer as the rational and objective service provider, and van Toorn argued that such objectivity is not only impossible but a disservice to society, as personal expression communicates much more powerfully.

While graphic design has since moved on from this debate, with both rational and personal expression holding credence, the debate still remains in the UX design field fifty years later. Objectivity is often considered to be ideal for UX design. Research methods (usability testing, ethnographic studies, card-sorting exercises, and more) are meant to result in an empirical and objective design in which the designer's personal preferences have been replaced by agreed-upon evidence. It's science.

Except it's not. Most companies selling design research are selling a pseudo-scientific con.

I have seen highly suspect conclusions from research studies where leading questions were asked to a ridiculously small number of people. I have also seen designers test the usability of their own products in such a way that the results always skew positive (see Principle 97). All this research is extremely expensive, takes a lot of time, and is often given greater importance than intuition and experience-based design decisions.

I'm not saying don't do research—we do research in our studio. But let's not pretend that the research is in any way scientific, or that it results in objective design. Research can help inform the design and remove some of your own bias, but it does not offer absolute truths (see Principle 53). The person who guides the research and interprets the results is still human and therefore unable to fully remove their own bias.

The emphasis on objectivity narrows our perspective and makes us less free, less open-minded, less creative, and less human in our thinking. I agree with van Toorn. Let's welcome the diversity of different personal and idiosyncratic perspectives. Listening to our intuition, acknowledging our past experiences, and bringing the totality of our human experience to the table is our greatest advantage as designers.

53

Most of the science in design is bullshit.

What makes a great design? Is there a way to measure it, quantify it, prove it? Is there a way to ensure it? The short answer is kind of, but not really. And that's not something that businesses like to hear. Most businesses don't want to invest a bunch of money into something that can't be proven. To placate their skeptics and get their work approved, designers have come up with snake-oil-salesmen-type research techniques to come up with numbers that will do the convincing for them.

It's what F.A. Hayek calls "scientism," and what the philosopher Karl Popper calls "the aping of what is widely mistaken for the method of science." The phrase "the research has shown!" exploits the extreme reverence businesses have for hard numbers, and since it's sold to people who cannot properly evaluate the research anyway, it's the quickest way to shut down any detractors.

So should we not do any research at all? No, we should. If we don't understand the end-user, we don't always know what to create. Learning about them and their context of use can help set focus and validate our decisions. But it will never be an exact science, and it won't show us what to do or how to lead.

In our studio, we start all projects by asking ourselves, our potential users, and our stakeholders a lot of questions. And let's be honest here; because we make biased decisions based on our own assumptions and intuitions, design research is not a science. It's a highly subjective discovery process. We are discovering things to expand our understanding. And that's OK. The fact that it's not quantifiable doesn't discredit the work.

Design takes courage on the client side as well as the designer's side. It takes courage to accept that good design emerges from a nonlinear, intuitive, and unreplicable—dare I say magical—process of a talented and empathetic designer (see Principle 52). And once we feel strongly about something as designers, it's more helpful to the success of the project to be able to articulate and argue that point than to hide behind "the research has shown!"

As designers, we need to be more honest about the complexity, creativity, and uncertainty involved in great design. Pretending that design is some sort of quantifiable hard science—which implies that it could be reproduced by whoever has access to the exact same data—actually does a disservice to the role of the designer and the process we go through to get to a great design.

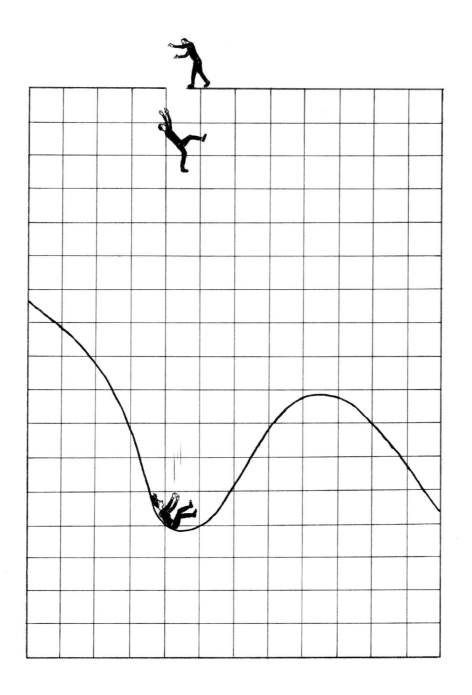

54

Do just enough research.

Understanding how much research to do, and when, really depends on the project. At one extreme is not doing any research at all, which would be a terrible idea since you would probably not be able to know what problem to even solve. At the other extreme is usability testing every single color, phrase, image, and design decision, which would take forever and give no space for intuitive design decisions.

As I am writing this, I am also teaching interaction design to master's students in Bangkok, Thailand. During the course, I break the class up into groups and give each group the exact same brief. The goal is for the students to go through just enough research to come up with a solution.

They are asked to come up with an idea for a native iOS app that will make backpacking through Thailand easier. The brief states that the app should solve a specific pain point that doesn't take the user out of their travel experience. The target audience is backpackers between the ages of eighteen and twenty-four, either traveling solo or with a group of friends, with a budget of less than $25 per day, and on a trip of two months or more.

Before they get started, students are given the following assumed pain points and are asked to validate and add to these pain points when talking to potential end-users later on:

1. Excursions can be too expensive when done alone.
2. There's no easy way to discover safe/healthy/cheap eats.
3. It's hard to get everyone to agree on what to do when traveling with friends.
4. It's hard to get in touch with local Thai people.
5. It's hard to get off the beaten path.

Once the students have received this brief and their questions are answered, their first exercise is to look at the current ecosystem of the company that sent them the brief (see Principle 55).

55

Map the ecosystem.

Digital products can exist by themselves, but they are usually part of a larger ecosystem. In the case of my students' backpacker app (see Principle 54), we imagine that the client's ecosystem also contains physical guidebooks and maps, a website, various social media channels, an app of common Thai phrases, and an itinerary-planning app.

It's important to start by analyzing all of the company's current products and the connections between them. That way we can get insights on how to leverage new and existing assets, understand whether or not there is a cohesive strategy across products, and identify what part of the ecosystem will be affected once the new product is added.

People turn to a variety of different products to accomplish different goals. What products within the ecosystem will users exclusively access through their mobile device? At what point will they turn to social media? What will they use the website for? And how about the physical products, or any of the other apps within the ecosystem? When do they come into play?

The great thing about ecosystem maps is that they showcase how everything is related from a bird's-eye view. It also serves as a bit of a mirror for the client, as it lays bare the overall product strategy (or lack thereof) on their end. Understanding how everything fits together before we start making suggestions is extremely important, otherwise we run the risk of duplicating existing functionality, or worse, cannibalizing important existing products within the ecosystem.

Because an ecosystem analysis encompasses the totality of a client's digital strategy, it's a very good place to start. We can come back to it when we need to start planning our competitive analysis, determine our user personas, prioritize features, or even figure out which user journey needs to be mapped out more clearly.

Once we have a firm understanding of the client's ecosystem, the next step that will deepen understanding is to look at any existing data, stats, or analytics the client can provide (see Principle 56).

56

Look at the data.

Once the ecosystem has been mapped (see Principle 55), it's time to look at the existing data and cozy up to the client's marketing department—the marketeers. Not all companies will have reliable data. That's because reliable data requires a stable product that's been in the market for at least a couple of years. Start-ups that have just released their first product, for example (besides not having a lot of extra money on hand to properly measure user behavior) will probably not have a stable enough user base to warrant investigation.

If we're lucky, the company's marketing department will have done a good job of keeping track of individual product performance and have data to look at. They'll be able to tell us what has and hasn't worked for their customers in the past and what they're planning to meet their business goals. If we're unlucky, the data sources will be chaotic, disorganized, or nonexistent. If that's the case, it's not the end of the world, and we'll have to close that gap with our own research.

When it comes to data, we typically ask for everything but the kitchen sink and create an online depository for the client to dump every possible piece of information or report they have on conversion rates, engagement, time spent in the product, feature usage, net promoter scores, previous campaigns, web traffic, new versus returning customers, brand awareness, SEO, Google analytics, digital marketing plans, device usage, cost per acquisition, ROI, and so on.

I don't claim to be a marketing expert, and most of it will not be super relevant to our project, but it's important to at least be aware of what is happening on the marketing side. Not because it's our job to optimize the marketing department's metrics, but because the reports and data can help paint a broader picture of customer and user behavior.

Besides reading through all the reports, I also do some online sleuthing. With the ecosystem in hand, I look at the reviews and comments for each individual product. That's usually where I have the most "aha" moments. It's amazing how much insight we can gather just by clicking through a handful of reviews for an hour.

It's important to note that data on its own is pretty much useless. It's not about gathering as much data as possible and calling it a day. It's also not about taking the data as law and basing every future decision on it. It's about helping us understand user needs on a holistic level prior to doing any user research ourselves.

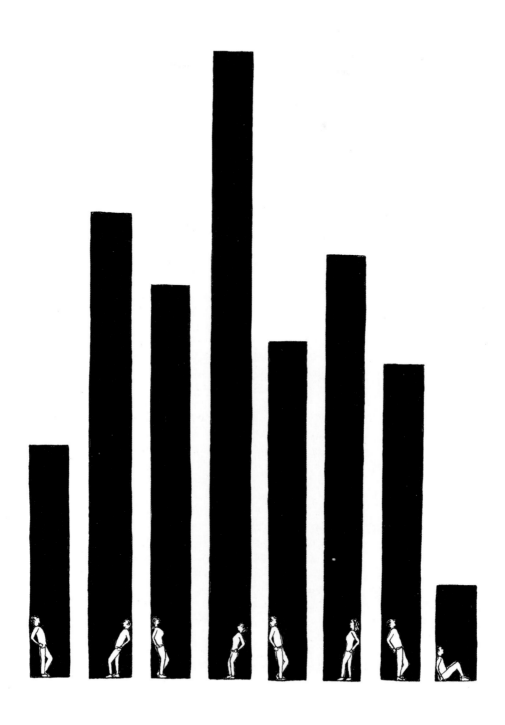

57

Not everything that counts can be counted.

William Bruce Cameron's 1963 text *Informal Sociology: A Casual Introduction to Sociological Thinking* contained the following passage: "It would be nice if all of the data which sociologists require could be enumerated because then we could run them through IBM machines and draw charts as the economists do. However, not everything that can be counted counts, and not everything that counts can be counted."

When it comes to doing user research, there are two ways of going about it. On the one hand, there's qualitative research that can't be counted—like observing behavior through ethnographic studies and interviews—and on the other hand, there's quantitative research—like surveys, A/B testing, and polls—that can be counted. Since humans, not numbers, tell us stories, qualitative user research is far more important in UX. Let's start there.

For the project where I ask my students to create an app that helps backpackers travel through Thailand, they have to observe backpackers in the wild, socialize with them, immerse themselves in their environment, and interview them. This allows the students to gain a realistic understanding of the backpackers' actual needs and pain points, not just their imagined ones.

First they have to set up shop somewhere on Khao San Road (aka Bangkok's backpacker central) and observe. That could be inside a hostel, on a busy street corner, or in a café. With pen and paper in hand, they have to write down their observations. For example: "Seems like all the bags are just tossed together. Storage? Safety? Convenience?" "People seem to be socializing much more and are not spending much time on their devices." "Long lines in front of the only information booth on the street."

This type of ethnographic research has its roots in anthropology and has been adapted by UX designers for user research and product development. And as with most UX deliverables, there is no right or wrong way of doing them. As long as we can reveal insights by understanding users in the context of their real-life environments, we're doing it right.

Once students have identified some pain points through observation, they can put together their interview questions (open-ended to allow for tangents), identify who would be good to interview (someone who is not busy), and find somewhere to conduct that interview (a place where everyone can sit down and hear each other). During the session, which are about thirty minutes, one student interviews while the other takes notes.

After about fifteen user interviews, students have to identify the backpackers' needs, habits, and attitudes and summarize and document their findings to come up with their hypothesis. Once that's done, they'll have to decide what they'd like to validate through quantitative methods (see Principle 58).

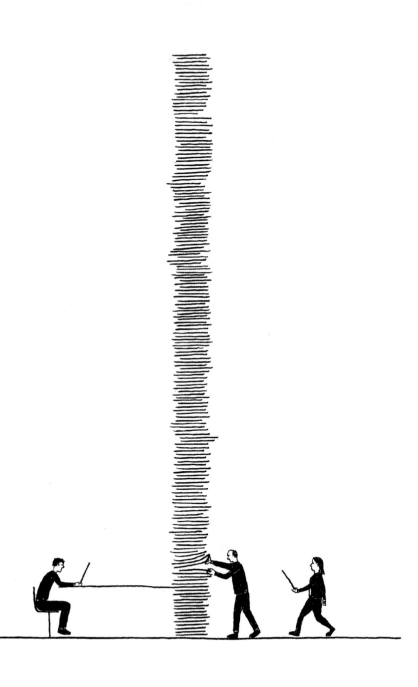

Research

58

Test for statistical generalizability.

Typically quantitative research is done when there's already a design or a product to test for usability. One example is an A/B test, which tests different layouts of a design to see which one performs better. Or we could use quantitative methods to understand what percentage of participants are able to successfully find a piece of information on a website and what percentage cannot. In both of these examples, the goal is to enhance the usability of an existing product or design.

Quantitative research can also be done at the start of a project, before we start designing and before there even is a product. It can be used to verify or debunk insights gathered during the qualitative user research phase (see Principle 57), test a hypothesis, or identify opportunities by generating numerical data that can be transformed into usable statistics.

Quantitative research at the start of a project is typically done by inviting anywhere between twenty-five to one hundred people who fit the target demographic to participate in a survey or poll. Fewer than twenty-five will make the results not statistically significant, and more than 100 will take too much time and cost too much money to perform. During the survey or poll, participants are asked specific questions to clarify some of the key themes that came up during the user interviews.

Let's go back to the student example (see Principle 54). Since at this point in their project the students have already identified the needs, habits, and attitudes of the backpackers through their observations and user interviews, it's time to test their findings or hypothesis for statistical generalizability by finding fifty backpackers to participate in their survey.

To measurable numbers, the survey questions need to be closed-ended with multiple-choice answers. "How important is safety when choosing a hostel?" (high/medium/low/no consideration) "How important is it to meet other travelers?" (high/medium/low/no consideration) Then once all participants have completed the survey, students can tally up the responses to see if the statistics match their hypothesis or the insights gathered during the user interviews, or if they tell a different story.

Quantitative research is about collecting data, employing the correct analysis, and presenting the results effectively. It can help differentiate between reasonable and dubious conclusions, provide deeper understanding, and convince business stakeholders who are used to making decisions based on hard data. However, it's important to never treat data as a rule of law, but only as something that supports our design decisions. Great design doesn't come from following the numbers; it comes from following our intuition.

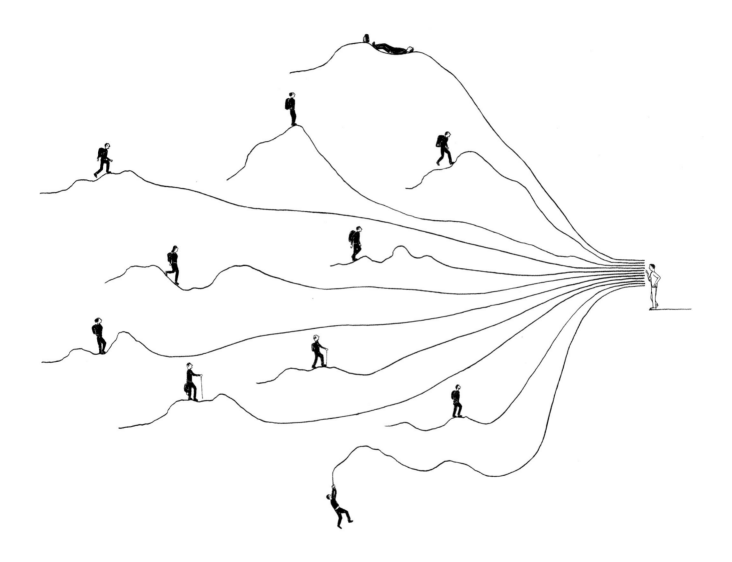

59

Don't base personas on assumptions.

"Eighteen-year-old Charlie is on her first month-long backpacking trip through Thailand with her two close friends from Amsterdam. She wants to experience as much as possible and tries to pack in as many sights and activities as possible. **She's not much of a planner** and usually goes along with whatever her friends want. However, **she hates wasting time**, and since she wakes up earlier than her friends, she would like to be able to **do things by herself** in the morning."

The above is an example of a fictional archetype, or persona, based on previously done research and real data, whose characteristics represent the needs, goals, behavior patterns, pain points, and attitudes of a larger group of real people. When done correctly, they can inform design decisions and help the team think through possible scenarios for specific features, for example, "How would Charlie experience, react, and behave in relation to feature X within the given context?"

Creating these kinds of behavior snapshots was first introduced in software development in the 1990s, but it wasn't until Alan Cooper's 1999 book *The Inmates Are Running the Asylum* that the term "persona" and the methodology behind creating them was properly defined. Since then, everyone—and I mean *everyone*—started creating personas, and that's where the trouble started, because it seems like not everybody knew what they were doing.

Over the course of my career, I have been handed some very cringeworthy personas that were based purely on speculation—or very shallow research—which included a ton of irrelevant information like their supposed hobbies, favorite movies, foods they like to eat, and relationship status. Who cares? This is not a creative writing exercise. I scream every time I have to read a 1,500-word biography that has nothing to do with the actual product.

But when the personas are based on ethnographic observations, user interviews, surveys, polls, marketing data, and usage data, they have the power to uncover previously unknown pain points, goals, needs, behavioral patterns, and attitudes towards the product. And because they help bring boring research to life, clients who are used to thinking of their customers as numbers are able to better empathize with the real-life human beings who will be interacting with their product (see Principle 1).

At their best, personas are a discovery tool for the UX team and a way to remind everyone else who's working on the product that we're doing all of this for actual people. However, it's important to always keep in mind that personas are there to help *inform* design decisions, not mandate them. Personas can help point us in the right direction, but they can't show us how to lead.

60

Keep your enemies close.

Whatever product or idea we come up with, it's very likely that someone else has already created something similar. Unless it's totally outlandish, it's almost impossible to create something that doesn't already have at least one, if not multiple, parallels. To make a product better than all the others, it's important to first scope out the competition.

First we need to figure out what it is that we are trying to compare. Are we interested in usability? Overall user experience? Specific features? Whatever it may be, determine the main comparison criteria and be sure to compare apples to apples to understand how the product stacks up against its competition.

Choosing between four and seven products to compare against is ideal. There's no exact wrong or right number, as long as it's not too few for the results to be myopic or too many so we end up with too much data.

Let's go back to the student example (see Principle 54). Let's say they are working on an app that makes it easier for backpackers to plan their activities as a group. In that scenario, they should identify all of their direct competitors in the travel space (apps that are specifically designed to help with planning group travel), while also looking at indirect competitors that allow for group planning across other verticals (like apps that help people split the bill).

Once the assessment criteria and the direct and indirect competitors have been identified, it's time to evaluate what makes each competitor unique, what the industry standards are, what features are shared across all, and where there might be space for innovation. Going through this exercise informs what it might take to gain a competitive edge and how to make a product that is better than all the others.

However, all data is only as good as the person analyzing it. And if the UX team is too busy looking at competitors, they might inadvertently end up creating something that is only marginally better but not actually innovative (see Principle 41). A competitive analysis clarifies what it will take to come up to par with competitors, but it does not show how to innovate and lead. Once again, that's where design intuition comes in.

61

Learn from bad examples.

We can learn a lot from products that are annoying to use; that's why it can be helpful to go one step deeper when looking at competitors and do a heuristic analysis of an entire flow. (Derived from the Ancient Greek word for "to discover," a heuristic analysis uses rules or educated guesses to find solutions to specific issues based on intuitive judgment.) Unlike usability, which tests how user friendly a design is with a variety of people from the target demographic, a heuristic audit is done by a UX designer (or multiple) to test the usability of an entire flow before designing.

Whenever I do a heuristic audit, I start by listing out which device or browser I am using to do the evaluation (as different browsers or devices can render information differently) and which task I am trying to complete (for example, return a product, order a car service, or claim bonus points). Then I go to the competitor's app or website and try to accomplish that goal.

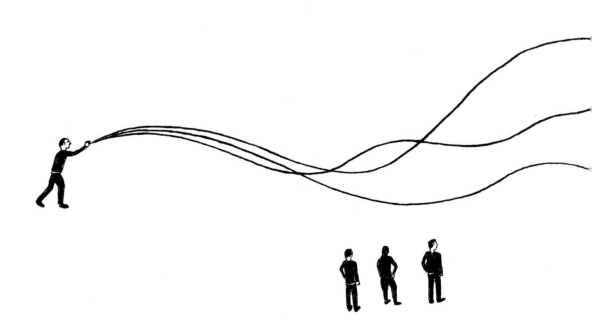

For this type of analysis, I am only interested in finding things that don't work, are annoying, take too long, interrupt me, confuse me, or block me from continuing. Things that work well, I ignore. When I do encounter a usability fail, I take a screenshot, put that screenshot into a Keynote deck, and rate each usability fail based on the following criteria:

- Visual design fail only (e.g., buttons that don't look clickable)
- Minor usability problem (e.g., buttons that are not in the most logical place)
- Major usability problem (e.g., too many different buttons with unclear labels)
- Usability disaster (e.g., inability to recover from an error)

Once I have done my evaluation, I either continue on to the next task I am trying to learn from or move on to the next competitor to see how they fare at the same task. Though I normally don't share the final result with other team members or with the client, I do make sure everything is documented in case I need to reference it myself later on.

Going through a competitor's flow is a quick and easy way to avoid potential friction points or usability issues in our own designs. By understanding where exactly competitors are falling short, we can design a superior flow or experience (see Principle 60). Plus, there's no need to make the same mistakes as others, right?

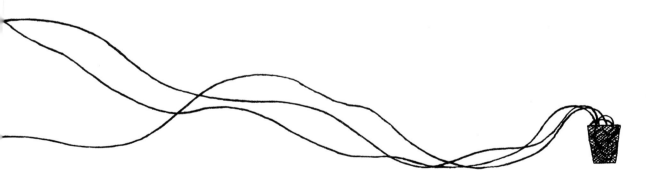

62

Make expectations work in your favor.

In 1943 Scottish psychologist Kenneth Craik proposed that people carry in their minds a small-scale model of how the world works, which they use to anticipate events and form explanations. These models of reality are constructed on personal life experiences, perceptions, and understandings of the world, and they allow us to filter and store new information to predict similar future events. He called these expectations "mental models," and this cognitive representation of reality is extremely important in the fields of UX and HCI.

Why? Because people tap into their existing mental models to interact with an interface. And those mental models are not only based on their previous experiences in the real world, but also they're based on all of their experiences with every single interface they have ever interacted with before. So to create something that feels effortless, it's important to understand how users conceive, categorize, and are inclined to act toward the physical and digital world around them.

When we were working on the Met Museum's website, we wanted to understand how people categorize not just the art but all of the other activities that were happening at the museum at any given time. We wanted to ensure that the design system we created—the global navigation in particular—would support people's existing cognitive representation of reality and would build on their preconceived notions and expectations, rather than forcing them to learn new ones.

But uncovering people's mental models is not easy. Since we designers are usually not the intended target audience, we can't make decisions based on our own mental models. And we also can't gain insights into people's internal representations of the world simply by asking them, because according to Argyris and Schön's "theories of action" research from 1974, what people say is different from what they do.

Mental models can be uncovered by applying a variety of UX research tools specifically designed to expose how people have constructed their understanding of the physical and digital world around them. My favorite method—card sorting (see Principle 63)—is the quickest and easiest way to get there.

63

Uncover consensus and ambiguity.

A card sort is a research method that allows us to uncover people's existing mental models to help design or evaluate the information architecture of a site. Card sorting involves creating a set of cards in which each card represents a concept or item and asking people to group the cards in a way that makes sense to them.

But before we get started with a card sort, we need to have a plan. How many people will participate? Will we be doing one-on-one sessions or group sessions? Where will we be doing it? What are we trying to learn?

Since the Met Museum was undergoing a complete overhaul of its entire existing information architecture, the goal was to understand how people categorize anything that is happening at the museum at any given time (see Principle 62). To get a good sample size of different mental models, both solo and group visitors were recruited for a total of twenty-five people across different ages and abilities.

Each of the eighty-five museum topics were written down on index cards, and participants were asked to categorize and organize all the cards into groups that made sense to them. If they had groupings with too many cards or too few, they were encouraged to break them down into smaller groups or combine them into larger ones. Once they were done, they were given a marker and an empty index card and asked to label their individual groups.

Throughout the exercise, they were reminded to share their thinking process out loud so we could understand if they were confident or unsure about their decisions. It also allowed us to hear how they referred to things, if certain groups were difficult to create, or if certain topics were difficult to put into groups.

Once all the card-sorting exercises were done, we put all the categories into a spreadsheet and highlighted consensus (labels and groupings that were created by most) and ambiguity (cards that were placed in various categories by different people). Then we used those insights to inform the design of the new global navigation system for the museum.

Seeing and hearing the way people organize information is a great way to step out of our own mental models. It also helps us understand how our users *expect* the system to function. Card sorts don't take a whole lot of effort, but if done right, the snapshot revealed helps us design a navigational system that not only anticipates the user's expectations but maybe even exceeds them.

→
Key screens showcasing the UI of the navigation of the Met Museum. It was based on the information architecture that came out of the card-sorting exercises done with actual visitors on the museum floor.

A bad user exp
can break ever
thoroughly bui
and an inappro
the power to in
people off.

rience
he most
brand identity,
riate UI has
tantly turn

64

Brainstorm efficiently.

Before the term "brainstorming" was recontextualized by advertising executive Alex Osborn in his 1948 book *Your Creative Power*, brainstorming meant you were having a sudden mental disturbance. That's why they almost called the method "thought-showering." They didn't, obviously, because I guess they realized that "let's go into the meeting room and thought shower" sounded more like you were cleansing your dirty thoughts and less like a method that allows teams to come up with many ideas in a short amount of time.

With the release of the book, the brainstorming method took the world by storm (no pun intended) and became a huge hit outside advertising as well. Every industry and organization introduced brainstorming as a way to generate ideas. From political strategies to aid work to coming up with new business ideas, all of it now starts with a brainstorm.

However, as anyone who's ever sat through an endless—and unproductive—brainstorming session knows, brainstorms can be a huge waste of time. That's because spending days with a group of unprepared people will get you nowhere. Sure, we'll have a wall full of sticky notes because "every idea is a good idea," but we're not going to have any real solutions.

To brainstorm successfully, we only need three things: an hour to think on our own, an hour to think as a group, and a sketchbook. That's it.

In our studio, whenever we start a project, Anton and I first read through the brief by ourselves. I try to formulate some sort of early problem statement to ground my thinking (see Principle 41), and we both try to come up with ideas before we discuss any solutions together. That's because it's better to walk into a brainstorm prepared with at least some ideas.

Then we take one hour to build on each other's ideas while sketching. Something Anton says might spark something in me, and something I say might make Anton think of something else. We've been doing it like this for years, but as I was researching for this book, I discovered there is a real scientific advantage to this method. Studies have indicated that to generate more creative solutions, we should sketch while talking, as it stimulates parts of the brain devoted to visual processing, giving us an additional creative boost.

When the hour is over, we summarize everything we just discussed and sketched, pull out the things that have potential, and go back to our computers to try to make it work. At the end of the day, we look at each other's progress and make concrete decisions and plans for design production that starts the following day. There's really nothing magical or complicated about it.

65

Build consensus.

If you ask 100 different studios about their process for showing their designs to a client, you'll get 100 different responses. Some will say it makes sense to involve clients as soon as the brainstorming stage to get their buy-in early—or even invite them to co-create—and others will recommend to show the client only near the finished UI design because they are not able to make decisions based on something that doesn't look real. Both are a bad idea. Here's why.

Let's start with agencies that get the client involved in a magical co-creation brainstorming workshop at the start of a project. They'll get their client to spend a couple of days putting sticky notes on a wall while eating fancy lunches on bean bags. Nothing really comes from it, obviously, but the thinking is that by spending a week or two playing pretend workshop, they'll be able to charm the client early on, hoping that it will give the creative team more autonomy in decision-making later on.

On the other extreme, there are the agencies who work secretly for weeks or even months, leading up to a grand-reveal presentation, where they show an entire flow in finished UI design to the client for the very first time. This approach also doesn't work, because without any previous buy-in or consensus building, designs are far more likely to get rejected.

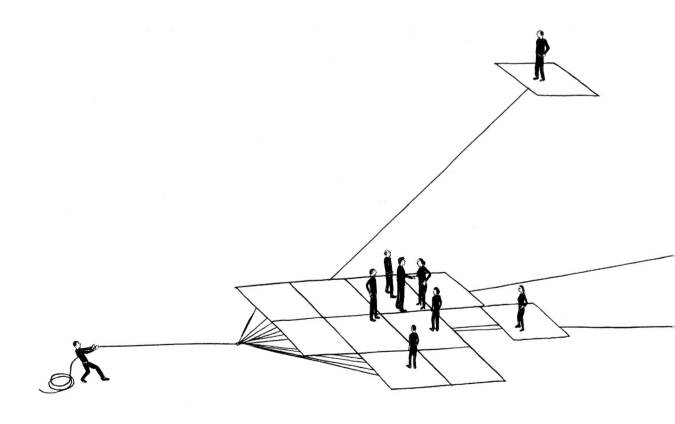

The truth is that getting buy-in is actually a lot simpler than that. All it requires is for us to communicate our design process clearly, indicate exactly where we need the client's input and why, and show the highest risk deliverables—the information architecture and five key screens in full UI design—as soon as possible. Once we go through that gate and get that signed off, trust is established and the rest of the project will go smoothly.

Showing how the brand will be applied in the first review meeting allows clients to imagine the final UI when they're looking at wireframes, which makes them more willing to provide sign-off based on wireframes alone. And that's the key, to have clients sign off wireframes during the remainder of the production period and not the visual UI design.

Why? If we get clients to the point where they feel comfortable discussing functionality in black-and-white wireframes that are easy to update, as opposed to visual UI design that takes forever to update, we can use the time saved on deliberately overdelivering on the UI design (see Principle 72).

This makes a huge difference. Having extra space in the project timeline to really go the extra mile on polishing the visual details will not only wow the client, but it will also impress the end-users, which is who we are really doing it for. Just make sure you buy yourself enough time to be able to do that.

66

Learn from real-world navigation.

We are surrounded by navigation systems all the time, when we walk into a subway, drive on a highway, find our way in a mall, find our gate at the airport, and so on. Even though the navigation systems that UX designers create are inside a computer screen, there is a lot we can learn by observing how navigation works (and doesn't work) in the real world.

At first glance, the Tokyo subway system appears overwhelming, but once you discover all the navigational aids, it's impossible to get lost. Besides identifying each subway line with a color and number, there are also color-coded guided paths painted on the floor you can simply follow until you get to your train. And once you're there, there's a diagram that tells you where the stairs, escalators, elevators, and exits are when you arrive at your station.

Amsterdam's Schiphol Airport is another example of amazing design. My absolute favorite one is that rather than relying on letters and numbers for its parking lot, Schiphol's parking has typically Dutch items like windmills, clogs, cheese, and tulips to not only make it easier to remember where you parked, but also to remind you that you landed in the Netherlands and nowhere else.

We can learn just as much from observing when navigation fails. Whenever you try to leave a French town by car, you are confronted with two signs pointing in opposite directions: *Toutes Directions* (all directions) and *Autres Directions* (other directions). What? French people know that "all directions" means highway and "other directions" means secondary roads, but it's not exactly intuitive.

The New Jersey Turnpike also presents us with a strange choice: express lane or local lane? And you better decide quickly, because you can't switch halfway through. The local lane is the only lane that has exits to smaller towns. So if you choose the express lane, but where you need to go is off a local exit, you have to drive all the way to the next express exit, switch to the local lane, and drive all the way back.

Every moment that we're in public, especially when we're in new surroundings or in a different country, is a great opportunity to learn about what works and what doesn't when it comes to navigation. And most of those things apply directly to designing a navigation system for interfaces as well (see Principle 67).

67

Build a logical structure.

Whenever we talk about structure in UX design, what we're really talking about is information architecture (IA), a term that was first coined by architect and TED conference founder Richard Saul Wurman in 1976. He thought changing the existing term "information design" to "information architecture" made it clearer that the focus of the practice should be on how a system works and performs, rather than what the system looks like.

In the digital space, IA is about the underlying structural organization that allows users to understand where they are, where they can go, how to find what they're looking for, and what they can expect (see Principle 68). The field pulls from library science (the study of categorizing, cataloging, and locating books and documents), cognitive psychology (the study of how the mind works and what mental processes take place there), and architecture (the process of planning, designing, and constructing structures). The result is the creation of site maps, hierarchies, categorizations, and navigation that form the foundation of the system.

An effective IA allows all users to easily meet their different goals through clear information hierarchy, labeling, categorization, and classification, which is known as the taxonomy. And since at least 50 percent of users will use a different entry point than the homepage and content is likely to grow, it's important to make sure that the structure has a variety of entry points and is scalable, modular, and extendable.

Why does all this matter? Because if people can't easily find what they're looking for, they'll either end up calling customer service—which carries a very high cost—or they'll just go somewhere else. They have alternatives now. Either way, they won't stick around to try to figure out your system. That is, if you've even made it to their search results in the first place. Google and other search engines actively punish poorly structured websites by ranking them lower in their results.

Similar to how a building can't be erected without a strong foundation, a digital product cannot be designed without a strong information architecture. And since we are now all living in the information age and spend more time on screens than we do sleeping, it's vital that the foundations of the digital places we call home are just as solid as our physical ones.

68

Visualize the relationship between pages.

All websites and apps are structured like Russian nesting dolls. As an example, let's take a marketplace-type website where you are trying to find headphones. The biggest doll, the doll that contains all other dolls, is the parent (homepage). When you open up the main doll, there's another doll inside (electronics), the child of the homepage. But inside that doll, there's another doll (headphones). And inside that doll, there is one final doll that can't be opened up and doesn't contain any other dolls (the actual headphones you were looking for).

What I've just described above is what we illustrate in a site map. A site map is a diagram that shows how the product's different pages relate to one another. It visualizes the information architecture and makes it clear how pages are organized and which sections contain other sections or pages. They're typically based on card-sorting exercises (see Principle 63) and user flows (see Principle 48), and they're meant to be a direct reflection of the target demographic's mental models.

Site maps are created at the start of the design process and are the first step toward the navigation that people interact with on the live product. It allows us to get a bird's-eye view of the entire information architecture and can help clarify which pages need to be trimmed or combined to simplify the structure, making it easier for people to find whatever it is they're looking for.

Each page on the site map has a label and a reference number. The label corresponds to the title of the actual page on the live product, and the reference number allows us to keep track of pages as we start wireframing. The headphones example could be visualized as follows:

0.0 Home
      1.0 Electronics
            1.1 Headphones
                  1.1.1 Headphone A
                  1.1.2 Headphone B
                  1.1.3 Headphone C

Having all the product page relationships displayed visually helps other team members like UI designers or developers understand the relationships between pages, making it easier to evaluate how and where to add a new page in the future. It's the blueprint of the information architecture, a living document that gets updated and referenced any time a change in the IA is required.

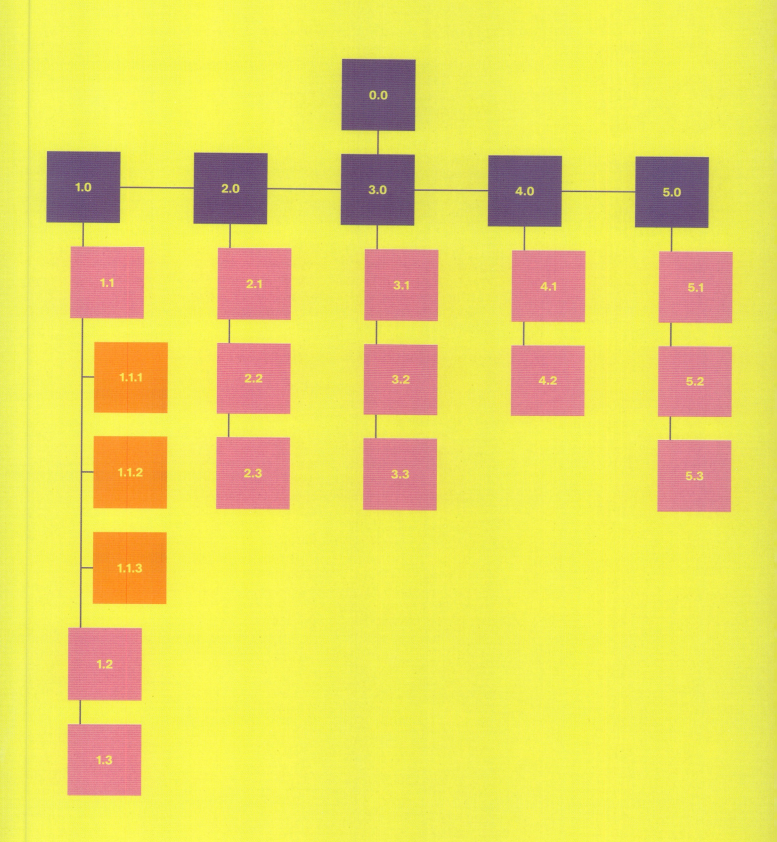

69

Don't get gimmicky with navigation.

The global navigation is almost always on the top left of the interface, the utility navigation on the top right (which typically consists of things like sign in, add to cart and search), and the footer on the bottom (which either repeats the global navigation or has items like contact and subscribe). This is not a coincidence. It's because the first interfaces were in English—which reads from left to right and top to bottom—and not in Chinese or Arabic.

The way we design interfaces—and what we are used to and what we expect—has changed quite a lot since the first websites of the '90s, but one thing has remained the same, the positioning of the navigation. Put a website from 1999 next to a website from today, and you'll see how the placement of the navigation is the only constant. Sure, the design of the navigation may have gotten a little more sophisticated, but if you strip away the design layer, the structure has remained the same.

That's because being too experimental or gimmicky with navigation can lead to people not understanding where they are, not being able to figure out where they can go, not knowing what to expect—and most importantly—not finding whatever it is that they're looking for. And if they can't find what they're looking for, they'll simply leave. So we've learned to be quite conservative with our navigation and stick to conventions.

And what are those conventions? Let's break them down.

1. Align navigation with the users' mental models.
2. Use language that is appropriate for the target audience.
3. Use meaningful and consistent labeling.
4. Flatten the structure as much as possible. (Keep subcategories to a minimum.)
5. Make it easy to scan.
6. Use colors or iconography as memory aids.
7. Make it clear what is clickable and what is not.
8. Allow users to easily exit, go back, and understand where they are.
9. Make the navigation accessible for people with visual, mobility, or hearing difficulties.
10. Consider entry from the side doors (i.e., not the homepage).

Navigation is the make-or-break part of user experience. If people can't find what they're looking for, or the user's goals and mental models have not been aligned with the navigation (see Principle 63), whatever else you've designed won't matter. People will be annoyed and leave. But if the navigation is intuitive, they are far more willing to forgive other hiccups in the user experience later on.

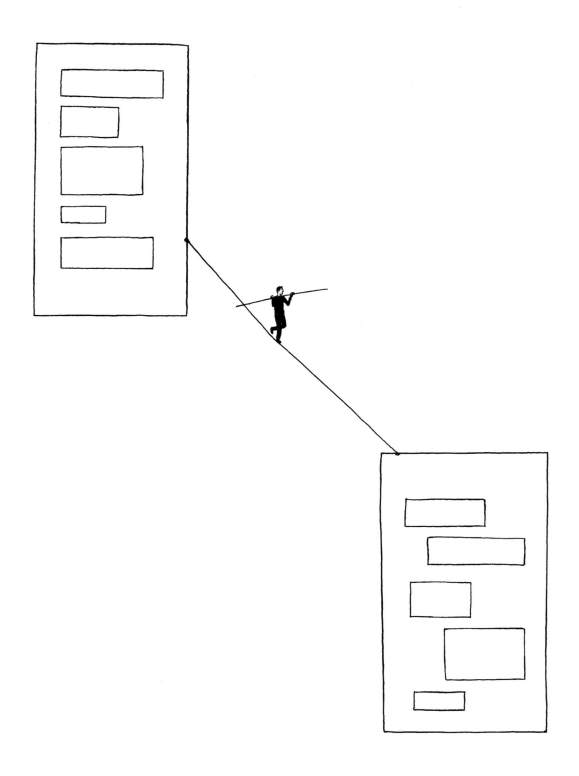

70

Yes, side doors matter.

Contrary to common belief, the homepage does not get the most views and is not the most important page of the user experience. It used to be, but it's not anymore, and it hasn't been for a long time. Nowadays, with more than half of a website's visitors first landing somewhere other than the homepage (and the vast majority of them never even seeing the homepage), it could even be considered the least important page of the user experience.

Think about the most recent time you went to a website. Did you type in the URL directly, or did you Google it and click on a link, or get there via social media instead? And when you arrived, did you land on the homepage, or did you end up on an interior page?

I always think of a homepage as the cover of a book that also happens to include the table of contents. Its job is to set the tone for what is inside and help people make decisions about what they'd like to do next. Whatever people decide to do next is where they'll actually be spending the majority of their time. That's why it's far more important to focus design efforts on the pages where people will hang out the most, rather than on the page that people will either never see or see once and then never again (Principle 15).

When we were working on the rebrand and redesign for talent-management company True Talent Advisory (which we renamed to True), side-door entry was extremely important. They have three distinctly different products with three distinctly different audiences, so we had to make sure that each product page received the same amount of design love that we would normally reserve for the homepage.

The goal of the new brand was to make True really stand apart from all of its visually bland and boring competitors. We ended up creating three distinct environments that were individually branded for each of their products. That way, regardless of where people landed, it felt unique, distinctive, and memorable.

So should we just get rid of the homepage altogether? No. Homepages still serve as the anchor of a site's taxonomy and help users reset and restart their path. But we should be clear that the homepage is just one of the many possible starting points of the user's journey, and not even the most important one at that. Unless the content frequently changes, we should aim to get people off the homepage as fast as possible so they can get to the content that actually matters to them quickly.

→
Since we knew the majority of people would bypass the homepage and land on an interior page first, we made each individual product landing page for talent-management company True as impressive as the homepage experience, while still making it all feel cohesive.

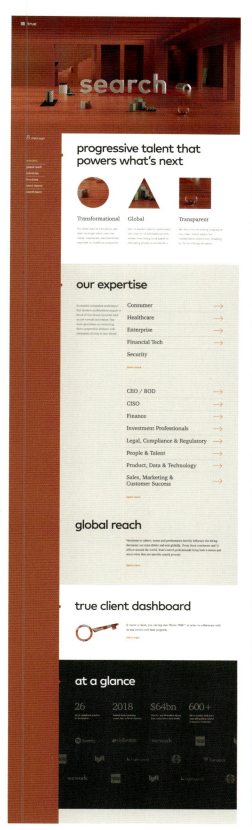

progressive talent that powers what's next

Transformational — Our large pool of executives and other strategic talent have the vision, experience, and functional expertise to transform companies.

Global — Our in-market experts understand the nuances of international tech sectors from hiring local talent to relocating people across borders.

Transparent — We share our recruiting progress in real time, which allows for collaborative experiences resulting in the best hiring decisions.

our expertise

Successful companies understand that modern professionals require a blend of functional expertise with an eye toward innovation. Our team specializes in connecting these progressive thinkers with companies driving to next ahead.

- Consumer →
- Healthcare →
- Enterprise →
- Financial Tech →
- Security

learn more

- CEO / BOD →
- CISO →
- Finance →
- Investment Professionals →
- Legal, Compliance & Regulatory →
- People & Talent →
- Product, Data & Technology →
- Sales, Marketing & Customer Success →

learn more

global reach

Variations in culture, teams and performance heavily influence the hiring decisions our teams make around the world. From three continents and 13 offices around the world, True's search professionals bring both a macro and micro view that elevates the search process.

learn more

true client dashboard

If you're a client, you can log into Thrive TRM™ at online to collaborate with us and review real-time progress.

client login

at a glance

26 — each in validated searches in all industries

2018 — fastest human-growing coach firm in North America

$64bn — Our VC and PE-backed clients have raised more such funds

600+ — We've worked with some fast-growing publicly traded tech companies and hundreds

helping leaders and teams reach their full potential

Assessment — Using narrative psychology we examine critical thinking to gain a clear understanding of individual and team dynamics.

Guidance — We believe in people's ability to improve themselves and their environments. All they need is the proper tools.

Growth — Positive change can last. Our personal proven plans are broken down into discrete experiences of lifelong growth.

our services

Our proprietary assessment methods allow us to discover drivers, biases for change and potential, which help clarify individual, team and organizational dynamics.

Selection — Identify which candidate is the best fit for the role and understand what kind of leader will complement your narrative team.

Executive Onboarding — Give new leaders the best chance at success from day one and help them keep momentum going.

Leadership Intelligence — Gain a clear picture of your leadership team's dynamics, culture, and the tensions and challenges affecting performance.

Due Dilligence — When investing in a company, determine how aligned the executive team is, what it mining and where the leadership risks lie.

Focus & Focus for Recruitment — Predict performance with our proprietary machine learning algorithms. Customized for organizations of 100+ employees.

Executive Coaching — Using agile people development methodology, we support leaders in achieving and sustaining professional growth.

Agile Action Plan Workshop — Gain tools for increasing team performance. Synthesize company strategy, context and team dynamics with leadership abilities and potential. Developed and led by typehome executive coaches.

at a glance

2017 — Founded in the US, and expanded to Mexico, Europe, UK, and Brazil

7 — At just ten countries, product has 24 product-market sell-togs

11 — We have worked with companies in 11 different industry sectors

400+ — Experts with actionable data on teaching & continuous evolution

news

Forbes 03/16/2019

How Walking In Darkness Teaches You To Handle Uncertainty. →

all news

shifting paradigms within our industry

Identifying Opportunities — We're always scanning our own workflows and structures to find spaces where we can innovate and lead in product development.

Sharing Solutions — Our products provide valuable insights into our own processes, and are designed to not only be used by us, but also by other companies.

Protecting Privacy — As each product functions in its own company, we emphasize data security ensuring there will never be any conflict of interest.

a history of innovation

Thrive TRM ® — In 2014 we built our first technology to create a better search experience for our clients. The cloud-based software made us more transparent, collaborative partners to our clients, and in each other, and matched data of change faster. Clients noticed and the software quickly caught on. Just one year later it was spun out as the flagship product for Thrive TRM, a new independent tech company for all recruiting firms, investment firms, and enterprises.

Synthesis Focus — We are on opportunity to help companies make restructuring decisions based on valuable data by creating a predictive technology that improves employees with leadership abilities and a strong culture fit. With the use of artificial intelligence, natural language processing, and machine learning, we provide data-driven insights to automatically rank employees' leadership potential. Armed with this knowledge, our clients can make promotions based on leadership potential and begin developing future leaders, which is especially useful during periods of growth.

news

The Philadelphia Inquirer 05/16/2019

Thrive TRM hires serial entrepreneur Lucinda Duncalfe to help the recruiting ...

all news

71

Prime before presenting.

"Thanks, everyone, for joining. We're about to look at our first round of wireframes. These wireframes are a skeletal, black-and-white representation of the content strategy, interactions, and information hierarchy that will appear in the final UI. Think of these wireframes almost as the paint-by-numbers version of our product. Besides labels and navigation items, all remaining copy you see is just placeholder, so don't worry about that. Once we have received your feedback on the items we will be discussing, we'll apply the brand, and you'll be able to see the wireframes come to life through color, typography, imagery, and design elements. Does anyone have any questions or comments before we get started?"

Even though clients have come a long way since I first started working as a UX designer and are now more familiar with wireframes, I still give this little spiel before presenting the first round. Sometimes there are people in the room from other departments who might not know what it takes to get to a digital product, and I want to make sure everyone understands what they're looking at.

I learned this the hard way. Sometime in the 2000s, we were working on the website of a smartphone manufacturer who was responsible for developing the first Google device powered by Android. We flew out to Taipei to present the first round of wireframes, and after I was done presenting, a hand went up, and one of our clients hesitantly said, "Eeeuhhhmmm . . . Irene . . . we want our website to be in English. Not in Latin. And also we would like it to be in color."

I did one of those "whaaa-whaa-whaaat" moves with my head and had to quickly backpedal and explain that the site will most definitely be in English and that the copy they saw was, in fact, just placeholder text called "Lorem Ipsum" (which is actually Latin dummy copy derived from Cicero's "De finibus bonorum et malorum") because we don't have the final copy yet, and that's not what we're reviewing today anyway, and haha, don't worry, of course the site will be in color, but we will get to that later.

It was a mess. And it was my fault for not realizing that most people are not familiar with the UX process and terminology I use daily. Ever since that meeting, I have made it a point to always set up each presentation with a little primer on not just what they're about to look at, but also what I expect from them in terms of feedback. It might be overly pedantic, but I'd rather be pedantic and crystal clear than run the risk of someone not understanding what I am talking about (see Principle 65).

Lorem ipsum dolor sit amet?

Lorem ipsum!

72

Move from low to high fidelity.

The fidelity of wireframes—the level of detail and realism—lies on a spectrum. On one end of the spectrum, there are loosely hand-sketched wireframes that show how the UI might work, and on the other extreme, there are detailed digital wireframes that visualize all content, visual hierarchy, and interactivity as close to the final UI as possible. Sketches can be done quickly, realistic wireframes are more time-consuming to produce, and in the middle, there are various levels of fidelity that require different levels of effort.

Low-fidelity wireframes are great as an internal thinking tool. Sketching gets overarching layout ideas on paper quickly, and changes can be made on the fly as thinking becomes firmer. Plus it puts the focus on what the interface should be, rather than on what it should look like, which can be a problem if we jump on the computer too soon.

High-fidelity wireframes are nice to show to users or clients. Since they look very close to the final UI, there's not much explanation required, making it really easy for people to react (see Principle 65). They're also a useful internal communication tool. The more detailed the wireframes, the faster the visual UI designer can go about their job, and the easier it is for the developer to understand how to implement the design.

In our studio, to go through the production process as efficiently as possible, we don't start working on high-fidelity wireframes until we have thoroughly explored and sketched out the interface. Once we have all the details ironed out, we invest time and effort in creating wireframes that look as close to the final UI as possible. And that's what we show to clients, not the sketches or visual design.

The reason why we want to receive final functional feedback on the wireframes is that updating the visual UI is much more time consuming. But to get clients comfortable with providing feedback on wireframes alone, we need to show them wireframes that are almost a paint-by-numbers version of the final UI so they can imagine what it might look like once the brand is applied.

→
Shown are the sketches, wireframes, and final UI of a product page for the Japanese pen tablet company Wacom. To go through the design phase as efficiently as possible, we asked the client to provide sign-off on the wireframes, not the final UI. That's why the wireframes look as close to the final UI as possible.

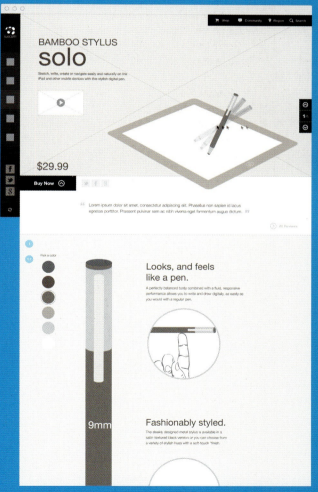

73

Don't just illustrate, annotate.

Annotations are written explanations accompanying a wireframe that describe how dynamic elements in an interface are supposed to function. For example, "On click, the dynamic menu panel opens" or "On tap, the user is taken to the corresponding detail page." Each annotation is paired with a numbered label on the design itself so anyone viewing the wireframes can easily cross-reference each design element.

Who is anyone? Well, quite a few people, actually. Developers will read the annotations to plan their workflow and understand how to build what. UI designers will use the wireframes to create production-ready designs. Collaborators, like motion designers, copywriters, or illustrators read the annotations to understand where their contribution is required. And clients use the annotated wireframes to provide feedback (see Principle 72).

Describing the functionality in words also helps verify all logic and thinking. It's very easy to accidentally overlook things like error states, edge cases, inactive states, hidden content, tool tips, logged-in states, or animations if they are not written down. Without annotations, it's very difficult to reference decisions and rationale on projects that were completed months or even years earlier, which is oftentimes needed as projects are paused or go into their next phase.

Despite this, almost every young UX designer I have ever had to mentor absolutely hated writing annotations and would either postpone or barely do them. And that's a terrible habit. Waiting until the very last minute to annotate all the wireframes can result in major holes in logic that, if spotted earlier, would not be a big deal to address. My advice is always to wireframe a screen and then annotate that wireframe before moving on to the next.

Well-annotated wireframes will answer every potential question to any audience, anywhere, at any time without the need to involve the UX designer. A developer on the other side of the world. A client in a different time zone. It also helps ensure all functionality is accounted for and allows us to refer back to our thinking weeks or months later. If done well, annotated wireframes help clear the way to a more efficient production process, saving a lot of headaches for everyone involved.

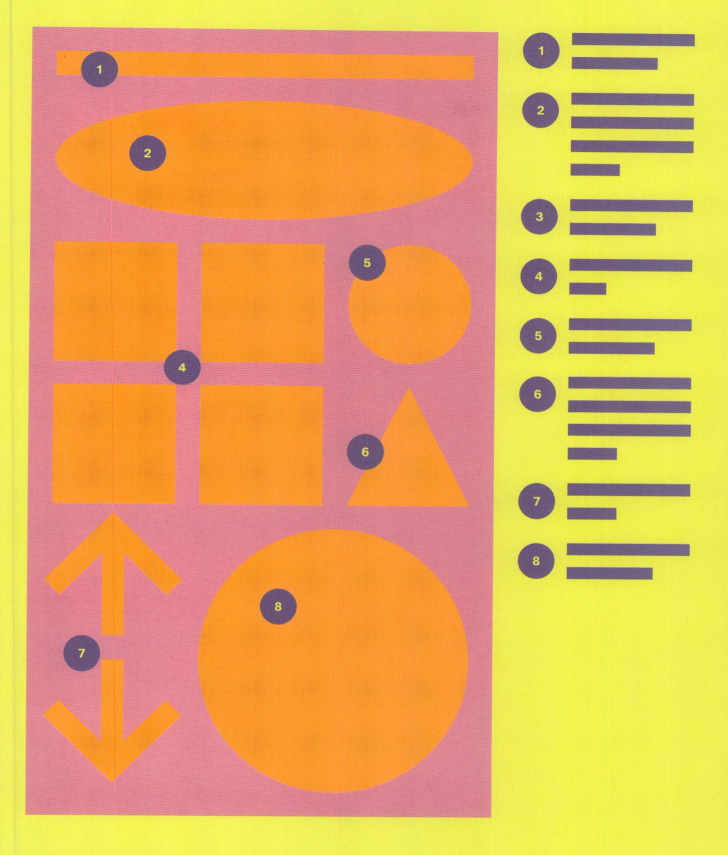

74

Interaction design is the brand.

Before we get too deep into UI design, I want to pause and talk about branding. We could fill a whole book (or many books) simply talking about branding, but I want to look at it from a UX perspective. If branding's job is to create a set of distinguishing features to promote awareness and recognizability of a product, then the UX and UI of the company's websites or apps are the most important vehicle toward influencing choice.

Why? Because 45 percent of people first encounter a brand through social media, 35 percent through the company's website—not through billboards, television commercials, or other traditional media channels like before. And since people are happiest when the digital product they interact with is attractive while simultaneously allowing them to achieve their goals (see Principle 8), the experience they have on digital channels becomes the cornerstone of the brand.

In our case, there are typically three ways in which we work with branding. The first scenario is when there's already an incredibly strong and recognizable brand in place, like when we work with Spotify. In this case, we have to carefully apply the existing brand guidelines to the UI and make sure the user experience matches the overall tone of the brand so it feels like part of the same family. For us, this is the least interesting because we're only really focusing on the UX, and the UI feels too much like paint-by-numbers.

The second scenario is when we work together with a traditional branding agency on creating a new brand from scratch across both digital and print, like we did when we worked with Mucho on the new brand for private equity firm Alpine. When every branding decision has to be validated across all possible channels, it results in the most robust brand identity possible, but it can also be hard to convey to a client that building an actual website takes much longer—and is much more expensive—than putting together print collateral.

The last and most common scenario is that there is no brand, or there's outdated branding that was designed for print. Start-ups, for example, tend to have limited budgets and prefer to spend their marketing dollars on their website or app directly, and more traditional companies might have branding elements that don't translate well to the screen. In both cases, the UX and UI end up becoming the brand.

Since a bad user experience can break even the most thoroughly built brand identity, and an inappropriate UI has the power to instantly turn people off, it's safe to say that in today's world, a brand is shaped by interaction design, not graphic design. Companies who understand that have the upper hand, and companies who don't, well, let's hope that they at least have some cool-looking business cards.

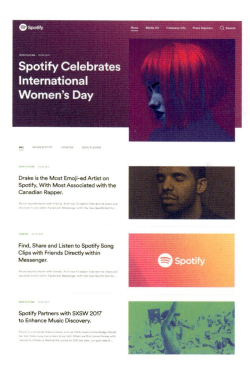
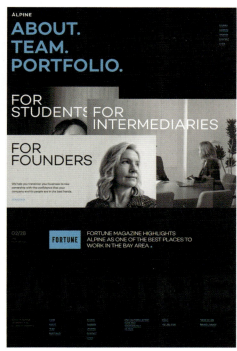

→
Key screens from our work with Spotify (where recognizable branding already existed), Alpine Investors (where we created the digital brand from scratch based on the print identity created by Mucho), and Markforged (where there was no real brand and the digital design ended up becoming the brand).

75

Bad typography leads to bad UX.

My favorite passage from Robert Bringhurst's 1992 book *The Elements of Typographic Style* emphasizes the power of typography: "Typography is to literature as musical performance is to composition: an essential act of interpretation, full of endless opportunities for insight or obtuseness. Much typography is far removed from literature, for language has many uses including packaging and propaganda. Like music, it can be used to manipulate behavior and emotions. But this is not where typographers show us their finest side. Typography at its best is capable of giving nourishment and pleasure in return."

Just like color, shapes, and music can evoke different emotions, so can typography. A design can go from old-fashioned to modern to chic by simply swapping out the typeface, making type an incredibly important branding element of the UI. But emotion isn't the only consideration when it comes to choosing type for a screen. Since many users will face different challenges based on their contexts, decisions in typography also have the power to make or break usability and accessibility (see Principle 18).

Maybe the person has vision difficulties, or maybe they are trying to read information in the glaring sunlight. Whatever the case may be, when you consider that type on a screen has to be usable first and beautiful second (especially considering the limited real estate available on mobile screens or even desktop computers), it becomes apparent that UI designers have to be far more conservative with their type choices than print designers have to be, since they don't face the same limitations.

Besides all standard good practices that also apply to print—like proper kerning (the spacing between letters) and leading (the space between multiple lines of type)—readability, scannability, and legibility are the most important considerations when working with type for a screen, as it leads to more accessible design. That's why it's better to err on the side of caution when it comes to type decisions, making sure text is never smaller than sixteen point and copy stays between sixty to eighty characters per line.

Since visual language and typography fall in the domain of the UI designer and play a tremendous role in influencing how people feel about an interface, it's incredibly important that the UX designer works closely with the UI designer for all type decisions every step of the way. Because if they don't and the typography is bad, the entire user experience will suffer. But if they do, there is a higher chance for the final interface to be as usable as possible to the widest group of people.

76

So you think you can scroll.

One of the most common UX myths is that people don't scroll. The number of times I've had to convince clients that we don't need to jam everything above the fold (the area first visible when landing on a website prior to scrolling) is ridiculous, especially since there's usability research from the UIE going back as far as 1998 that shows people didn't mind scrolling even back in the '90s. In fact people much prefer scrolling over clicking interactive elements when it comes to revealing additional content.

Scrolling means "I am interested in more," whereas clicking means "let me move on to something else." But scrolling through long paragraphs of static text can also lead to scrolling fatigue. That's where *scrollytelling* comes in.

"Scrollytelling" is a term that describes the combination of scrolling and storytelling and is used to help people stay engaged in long-form content or complicated data visualizations (see Principle 78). Rather than taking people out of their experience by making them click on tool tips, videos, or image galleries, scrollytelling dynamically reveals content, animations, sound, and image transitions as the user scrolls up and down the page.

The *New York Times* is often credited with inventing, or at least popularizing, scrollytelling. Back in 2012 they published the Pulitzer and Peabody Award winning story "Snow Fall: The Avalanche at Tunnel Creek," where the elements that appeared on scroll formed a flowing, captivating story in motion. Soon after, scrollytelling became one of the most common ways to create an immersive browsing experience in long-form journalism, brand homepages, product pages, and creative portfolios (our own included!).

Good scrollytelling allows the user to control the pace of the animation and creates a strong connection between content and motion that has the power to make the journey more enjoyable than the final destination. But we have to be careful. Bad scrollytelling (or scrolljacking) can create a jarring misalignment between the animations and the story, which can make the entire experience feel gimmicky and annoying. Make sure you know what you're doing.

→
For the promotional website of our self-initiated UrbanWalks iOS app that provides walking tours in New York City, we used the top view of a New York City taxi cab to help guide users down the page. Users were able to control the speed of the taxi—and therefore the pace of the story—simply by scrolling down.

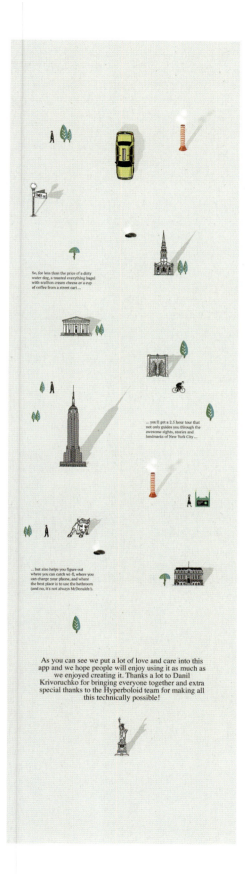

So, for less than the price of a dirty water dog, a toasted everything bagel with scallion cream cheese or a cup of coffee from a street cart ...

... you'll get a 2.5 hour tour that not only guides you through the awesome sights, stories and landmarks of New York City ...

... but also helps you figure out where you can catch wi-fi, where you can charge your phone, and where the best place is to use the bathroom (and no, it's not always McDonalds!).

As you can see we put a lot of love and care into this app and we hope people will enjoy using it as much as we enjoyed creating it. Thanks a lot to Danil Krivoruchko for bringing everyone together and extra special thanks to the Hyperboloid team for making all this technically possible!

So, for less than the price of a dirty water dog, a toasted everything bagel with scallion cream cheese or a cup of coffee from a street cart ...

... you'll get a 2.5 hour tour that not only guides you through the awesome sights, stories and landmarks of New York City ...

... but also helps you figure out where you can catch wi-fi, where you can charge your phone, and where the best place is to use the bathroom (and no, it's not always McDonalds!).

77

Animate responsibly.

The first example of a functional animation in an interface goes back to 1985, when Brad Myers presented a paper on "percent-done progress indicators," which found that when the computer provides a visual cue about its progress on a task, the experience of waiting becomes more bearable to users. This research gave birth to the progress bar and all other functional animations that followed.

Decorative animations, on the other hand, serve no real functional purpose. When done effectively, they attract the user's attention and tell a story, but when done poorly, they can be annoying, distract users from their goals, and prevent them from completing their task.

When we were working on our self-initiated and self-funded interactive documentary *One Shared House*, about my experience growing up in a communal house in Amsterdam, we wanted the homepage to look like a movie poster. Since the story is about my childhood, we wanted it to feel as if I was looking back in time as an adult to a crucial moment in the film where the communal dinners are no longer taking place, signaling the end of the communal dream.

We bought some Barbie furniture and a plastic box from Muji, 3D printed some tiny furniture, and spray-painted everything to the purplish-blue violet of our color palette, with the exception of one chair—my chair—which we spray painted pink. We then set up the lamps and shot everything in camera and created a stop-motion sequence that would be triggered on mouse movement. My eyes followed the user's mouse, and my chair would drop as soon as the user indicated they wanted to start the documentary.

Though these animations served no real functional purpose, they created continuity that had previously been lacking between the homepage and the interactive film. It also brought the interface to life and added a unique and distinctive visual element to the overall experience, which helped tell a more cohesive story (see Principle 74). And since people ended up playing around with the reaction of my eyes to their mouse, they spent way more time on the homepage than they would have otherwise.

UI animations have the power to attract the user's attention, but that is also their biggest disadvantage. Whereas functional animation should be invisible and unobtrusive, decorative animation should be anything but that. However, no matter how subtle or eye-catching, animations should never get in the way of usability. Before we introduce them to the interface, we need to first consider the value each animation brings to the end-user and remember that the animation should add something to their experience, not get in the way of it.

→
The homepage of our self-produced interactive documentary *One Shared House*, about my experience growing up in a communal house in the center of Amsterdam. My eyes follow the user's mouse cursor, and when they select "watch the documentary," my chair—the pink chair—drops.

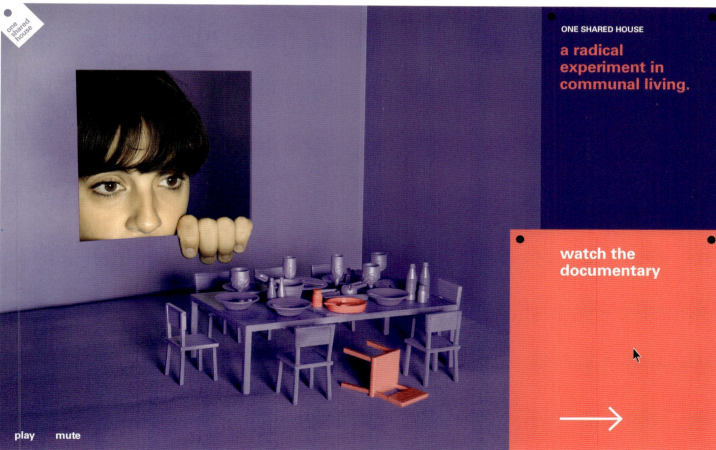

78

Make data lovable.

When people hear "data" or "data visualization," they tend to think of charts, graphs, spreadsheets, or something abstract and boring that has to do with statistics. And even though its intended purpose is to make big numbers feel more comprehensible, many data visualizations do the opposite.

Earlier in this book, we talked about how visual metaphors have the power to help audiences relate by tapping into existing symbolism (see Principle 7). And if there is one thing we need help relating to, it's big data and large numbers.

In 2009 we worked on a project with advertising agency Cramer-Krasselt for Porsche that introduced their first four-door sedan, the Panamera, to the North American market. Most car websites at that time were just flashy showcases of features and details, but we wanted to celebrate the fact more than 70 percent of all Porsches ever built are still on the road. (Porsches, like heirlooms, tend to stay in the family for generations.)

We created a user-generated library of thousands of stories submitted by Porsche owners and fanatics—even Jerry Seinfeld submitted some stories—which we visualized in the form of an interactive family tree. Stories submitted from the West Coast were on the left side of the tree, and stories from the East Coast were on the right. Older Porsche model stories were on the bottom, while newer Porsche models were at the top.

With the family-tree metaphor being fairly easy to grasp, people intuitively knew how to interact with the interface, creating a more immersive experience with the actual data that powered the interface without much effort. It also allowed them to feel like the data they submitted made them part of the larger Porsche family.

It's important to keep in mind that not all data needs to be visualized. As we are now in the era of big data, it's tempting to turn everything into a data visualization. But before you start thinking through how to visualize the data in front of you, make sure that the data is actually relevant and interesting to your intended target audience, because nobody is interested in data for data's sake.

Add your story to the Family Tree

There are as many Porsche legends as there are people who love the cars. And this is the place to see them all. Explore the family and its stories and add your own contribution to our written history.

ADD YOUR
PORSCHE
STORY

ALL MODELS ▲   1950-2010 ▲   ALL STORIES ▲   ALL AREAS ▲   ALL ITEMS ▲   Search 🔍

Panamera
Welcome to the family.

Dealer locator   Legal Notice   Privacy Policy   porscheusa.com

WHICH PORSCHE ARE YOU?   START ▶

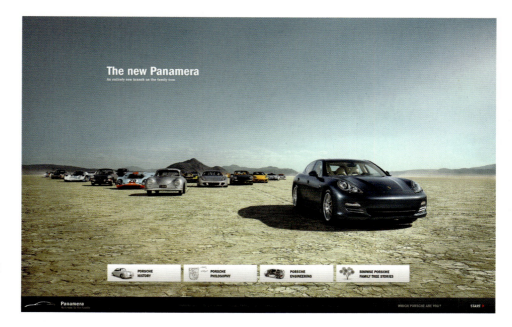

The new Panamera
An entirely new branch on the family tree

PORSCHE HISTORY   PORSCHE PHILOSOPHY   PORSCHE ENGINEERING   BROWSE PORSCHE FAMILY TREE STORIES

Panamera
Welcome to the family.   WHICH PORSCHE ARE YOU?   START ▶

→
Key screens from the Porsche Panamera website we worked on in 2009. Stories from the West Coast are on the left side of the tree, and stories from the East Coast are on the right. Older Porsche model stories are on the bottom, and stories about newer Porsche models are at the top.

Design

79

Dark mode rises.

Dark mode refers to a type of screen display that has light text on a dark background, also known as "negative polarity." Light mode, on the other hand, has dark text on a light background, which is "positive polarity." Light mode has been the dominant display type for almost thirty years, but dark mode is making a big comeback recently with claims of prolonged battery life, improved readability, and reduced blue-light exposure. Plus, it looks cool. So which is better? Well, it depends.

All developers I have ever known code in dark mode. They claim that dark mode is easier on the eyes when you have to stare at a screen all day because it emits less blue light. They also say lines of code stand out more against a dark background, and reading lots of text on bright displays causes more eye strain when working in a dark room. They're not wrong—that's all true and backed up by science.

However, most people in most scenarios prefer light mode. Disregarding our evolutionary preference of having dark images on top of a bright background—we are not nocturnal animals, after all—it's much easier to read long lines of text in light mode. That's due to the halation effect, which blurs the edges of bright text when it's on a dark background, making longer passages of smaller text more difficult to read.

So what should we do? It depends on the purpose of the content and the context of use. Dark mode is better for emphasizing visual content (think Netflix covers) and short blurbs of text (like lines of code). It's also better for our eyes when we're viewing content on the screen in a dark room. Light mode makes it much easier to read long paragraphs of text and to view content on the screen during the day.

If we want to draw attention to visual content, dark mode is a safe bet. If we want people to read, light mode is better. When in doubt, we can always offer both and have the user choose for themselves. But whatever you do, make sure your decision is based on context of use, not based on what you think *looks* cooler.

One morning, when Gregor Samsa woke from troubled dreams, he found himself transformed in his bed into a horrible vermin. He lay on his armour-like back, and if he lifted his head a little he could see his brown belly, slightly domed and divided by arches into stiff sections. The bedding was hardly able to cover it and seemed ready to slide off any moment. His many legs, pitifully thin compared with the size of the rest of him, waved about helplessly as he looked.

"What's happened to me?" he thought. It wasn't a dream. His room, a proper human room although a little too small, lay peacefully between its four familiar walls. A collection of textile samples lay spread out on the table—Samsa was a travelling salesman —and above it there hung a picture that he had recently cut out of an illustrated

14

Metamorphosis

One morning, when Gregor Samsa woke from troubled dreams, he found himself transformed in his bed into a horrible vermin. He lay on his armour-like back, and if he lifted his head a little he could see his brown belly, slightly domed and divided by arches into stiff sections. The bedding was hardly able to cover it and seemed ready to slide off any moment. His many legs, pitifully thin compared with the size of the rest of him, waved about helplessly as he looked.

"What's happened to me?" he thought. It wasn't a dream. His room, a proper human room although a little too small, lay peacefully between its four familiar walls. A collection of textile samples lay spread out on the table—Samsa was a travelling salesman —and above it there hung a picture that he had recently cut out of an illustrated

14

↑
Examples of light mode (left) and dark mode (right) with passages from Franz Kafka's book *The Metamorphosis*. For most people in most contexts, light mode is preferred when reading long passages of text. But dark mode better emphasizes imagery.

80

Never give total control.

The more flexible the interface, the more control the user has. But the more control the user has, the more complex the interface becomes. The amount of control we want to give really depends on the intended target audience. If the product is meant to be widely adopted, users should be somewhat limited, but if the product is meant for highly specialized professionals, it's better to give as much control as possible.

Basic control and flexibility that allows the user to easily go back, cancel, close, or undo is a given and should be supported in any interface. But allowing users to completely customize their experience should be reserved only for professionals or not given at all. The happy intermediary, where everyday users have enough flexibility that they're able to self-publish or determine their preferences, but not too much control that it makes the tool overly complex, is usually the sweet spot (see Principle 46).

Let's take our clients at the Art Directors Guild as an example. ADG, as it's colloquially known, is made up of art directors, set designers, illustrators, and graphic artists who work in film and television. Some of the guild's members use extremely complex and highly customizable software on a daily basis, whereas others barely ever touch a computer at all in their daily work. We had to make sure the system we designed worked for both (see Principle 19).

For the new digital home of all ADG members, the only place we gave them control was in their own profile section. Members could list their skills and contact information and upload images from their portfolios or stills from productions they had worked on. We also gave them control over what information they wanted to make public to everyone and what information they wanted only fellow members to see. That was all the control they were given.

As designers it's our job to determine the sweet spot between flexibility and control. If the intended target audience is very technically sophisticated or uses the interface professionally, more control—but never total control—should be given. But if we're designing an interface that should be accessible to every Tom, Dick, and Harry, we need to be very clear about what level of control we want to give them and why. Otherwise we run the risk of creating unnecessarily complicated tools full of power features nobody ends up using.

→
Members of the Art Directors Guild—a labor union representing film and television professionals—are able to control whether or not their profile page is public. They can also add their bio, contact information, skills, work experience, productions they worked on, what locations they have experience working in, and what recognition they have received. They can't, however, control the design of their profile page.

ADG

RYAN GROSSHEIM

ASSISTANT ART DIRECTOR - FILM

SEND E-MAIL
IMDB PROFILE
WWW.RYANGROSSHEIM.COM
TUMBLR.RYANGROSSHEIM.COM
PDF RESUME

AGENT: DAN BROWN
AGENCY: BROWN LLC
AGENCY PHONE: 123-456-6788
AGENCY CELL: 123-456-6788
E-MAIL AGENT

✕

YOUR PROFILE IS SET TO **PUBLIC**   CHANGE

CHANGE PASSWORD

Ryan Grossheim is a Production Designer & Art Director for film/television based in southern California. He also works as a scenic designer and concept artist for themed entertainment and theatre with clients including the San Diego Zoo.

SKILLS

Scenic Painting: Theatrical
Computer/Design: Adobe Illustrator
Computer/Design: Adobe InDesign
Computer/Design: Adobe Photoshop
Computer/Design: Vectorworks
Drafting/Models: Foamcore Models

Drafting/Models: Finish Models
Title/Graphics: Logo Design
Title/Graphics: Production Graphics
Computer/Design: AutoCAD (AutoDesk)
Computer/Design: SketchUp

EXPERIENCE

Extensive Experience in Design for Theatre and Themed Entertainment

MFA - Design & Technology - San Diego State Dept. of Theatre, Television and Film

Lorem ipsum dolor sit amet, consectetuer adipiscing elit. Aenean commodo ligula eget dolor. Aenean massa.

Mac and PC proficient

RECOGNITION

Emmy Award for Hairspray Live!

ADG Nomination for Hairspray Live!

Emmy Nomination for The Voice

ADG Nomination for The Voice

LOCATION EXPERIENCE

Los Angeles, Boston, Chicago

CREDITS

ADD CREDIT

NETFLIX

MINDHUNTER
SEASON 1, 2
ASSISTANT ART DIRECTOR
👥 3

THE GOOD PLACE
SEASON 1, 2
ASSISTANT ART DIRECTOR
👥 4

HAIRSPRAY LIVE!
ASSISTANT ART DIRECTOR

81

Personalization is hit or miss.

If customization is about giving users control, then personalization is about giving that control to the system to make decisions about what it thinks the user wants based on previous behavior. There is a fine line between using data to get to know our user better and using data to stalk them. There's an even finer line between being spot on with a recommendation and being totally off.

Personalization based on data that is explicitly and knowingly given by the user, like surveys or forms, is totally benign. But when we personalize content based on data that users probably didn't even realize is being collected on their behalf, like location or device data, it's getting a bit stalkerish. And when we start making recommendations based on the user's behavioral patterns, it starts to get icky.

When Spotify allows us to discover new music we love, or Netflix has the perfect suggestion on what to watch next, it can feel magical. But when the system infers that a user is pregnant based on searches and recent purchase history and then inundates that user with ads for baby products—months after the very real woman on the other side of the screen has miscarried—it's not just a miss, it's traumatizing. And yes, this has actually happened. It also lays bare that all this targeted content based on months (or sometimes even years) of data gathering isn't quite as smart as we think.

According to a report by customer engagement company Twilio, 69 percent of people say they are fine with personalization—as long as it's through data they've shared directly and knowingly. So the ethical way to collect data is to first ask for the user's consent. The problem, however, is that most companies don't ask, and when they do, most people don't read the fine print (see Principle 14).

The real question here is, does past or current behavior necessarily indicate future desire? We all appreciate discovery and exposure to the unexpected, but when things track too closely or we feel like alternatives are being hidden from us, it's annoying.

For me, I would like to be able to opt in or out of sharing my data whenever it suits me. For example, writing this book has destroyed years of carefully collected data on my music-listening behavior because I can write only while listening to background jazz. So now my favorite digital product of all time—Spotify Discover Weekly—is completely ruined because it recommends only more background jazz, which will take years to recover from.

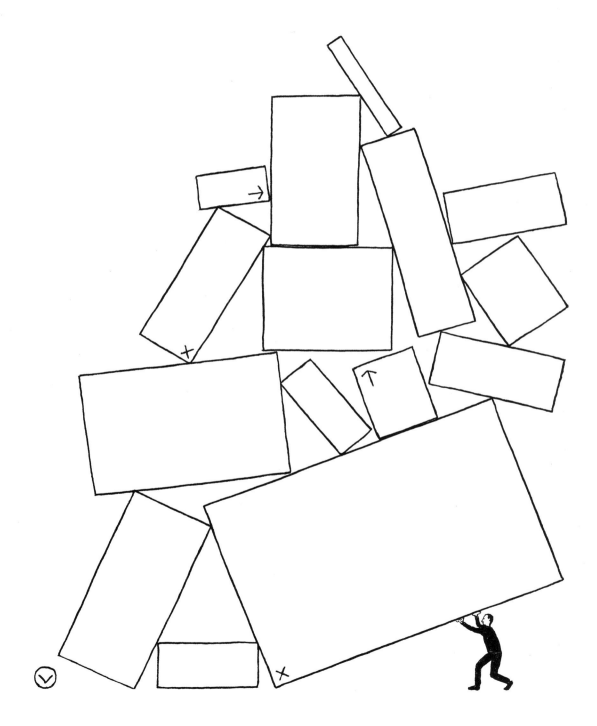

Design

82

A word is worth a thousand pictures.

Even though I've been writing emails for more than twenty-five years, I still confuse the "attach a file" icon with the "insert a link" icon about 50 percent of the time. I'm also afraid to change the settings on my washing machine because I have no idea what any of the other icons mean, and I'm too lazy to look it up in the manual. And any time an icon starts flashing on my car's dashboard, I have no idea how concerned I should be, as I have no idea what it could possibly mean.

And it's not just me. The UIE conducted two experiments to better understand our relationship with icons. When they changed what the icons looked like but kept them in the same location, users were able to adapt and perform their tasks without much additional effort. But when they kept the design of the original icons and shuffled their locations around instead, people got so confused, some couldn't even complete the most basic tasks. So people remembered where the icons were located, but not what they looked like.

The problem with icons is that very few are so ubiquitous that they don't need a descriptive label. So, few in fact, that I can list them out right now: a house for home, printer for print, magnifying glass for search, cogwheel for settings, heart for like, folder for files, letter for mail, speech bubble for chat, pencil for edit, spinner for loading, bell for notifications, trash bin for delete, shopping cart for add to cart, camera for photos, pin for location, lock for secure, arrow for play, and a silhouette for user profile.

Outside of these examples, almost all other icons—including the hamburger menu icon—have the potential to be ambiguous to at least some users. Not because it's not metaphorically representative of something the user can relate to in the real world, but because its meaning is different across different interfaces. Let's take the star icon as an example. Does tapping the star mean we're saving it for later, or does it mean we're rating it? Depends. This lack of standardization is like trying to learn a language where the meaning of the words keeps changing depending on who's talking.

At their best, icons are easily recognizable, save space, are aesthetically appealing, make good touch targets, and are language agnostic. They also have the ability to make a design system feel more cohesive and recognizable. At their worst, however, they're superfluous, hard to decipher, and harmful to the overall user experience. When in doubt, it's best to always accompany an icon with a text description, and if you can't, at least keep them in an expected location so users will know where to look for them based on muscle memory alone.

83

Understand the sales funnel.

An average Joe buying something is referred to as B2C (business to consumer), whereas companies buying entire solutions are referred to as B2B (business to business). The reason it's important to distinguish between the two—especially when it comes to e-commerce—is that the goals of a consumer versus a company are different. Consumers might make a purchasing decision in fifteen minutes or less, while companies will first go through a long research, evaluation, and negotiation process before settling on a partner or vendor.

Let's take the project we worked on for Markforged (manufacturer of industrial-grade 3D printers in the B2B space) as an example. Their sales cycle is much longer than the sales cycle of a company who makes 3D printers for personal home use. That's because switching an entire manufacturing process is a much bigger and riskier decision than choosing a 3D printer that lets you print a plastic Yoda at home.

Another big difference is that e-commerce is never as simple as "add to cart" in the B2B space. In fact, you almost never see prices up front. And if you do, they're usually approximate. Pricing in B2B is based on the volume of purchase and level of technical support or system integration required, so it's almost always negotiable. Most B2B companies—Markforged included—have entire sales teams ready to discuss a potential sale, and that process still happens in the old-school and hyper-personalized "let me give you a call" kind of way.

But before they decide to call, companies first shop around and scout their options online. That research is typically done by an entry-level employee who collects things like whitepapers, videos, testimonials, technical specs, and demos to build a case for their manager. Then the manager will look at the options and evaluate which solutions best match their needs, narrowing the list to a handful of potential partners or vendors.

For Markforged, our goal was to support the entry-level employee with their research. The better they were able to do their research, the higher the chance that Markforged would make it to the short list. If Markforged would have been selling directly to consumers, our approach would have been totally different. In that case, our goal would have been to get the user through the purchasing process as quickly as possible.

Though the approach differs, all the rules that make up good UX—clear information architecture, high usability, great aesthetics and branding, short paths to the user's goals, and well-organized, relevant product information—still matter (see Principle 74). That's because companies are made up of regular Joes who interact with B2C interfaces all day long. Just because we're selling straight to companies doesn't mean we get to skip out on covering the basics.

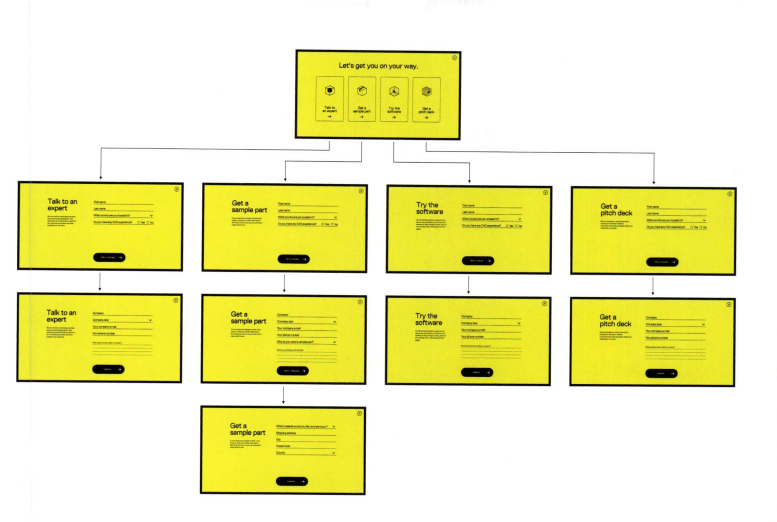

↑
Rather than pushing users through the sales funnel, the goal
for Markforged was to help people better understand the
company's offering.

84

Target the right devices.

According to Statista, only about half of households worldwide have a desktop computer, but about 75 percent of the world's population now owns a smartphone. That divide grows wider each year. With smartphones accounting for about 60 percent of all internet traffic worldwide, creating a design system that takes mobile interfaces into consideration is a no-brainer.

This makes mobile interfaces extremely important. In 2009 Google product designer Luke Wroblewski argued that to reduce the amount of overly complex functionality in mobile interfaces, we have to design for "mobile first," not just simply scaling everything down from desktop, which is what everyone was doing up to that point.

However, the problem with a mobile-first design approach is that it often means mobile only. The interface will look great on mobile devices, but awkward and empty on desktop computers. It also means that when new and even smaller devices are introduced into the ecosystem, like smartwatches, we end up with the same problem: The design can't scale down.

It's important to keep in mind that the way we interact with devices is not the same. Mobile devices are in our hands and with us at all times. We use them when we're bored or to get us where we need to go. Desktop computers, on the other hand, are mostly used at home or at work for activities that require more focus and precision.

And just because the majority of the world is accessing the internet from their smartphones doesn't mean the majority of our actual users are as well. Rather than designing for one device first, it's better to have all the devices that are actually being used—desktop, mobile, tablet, and whatever else—on the table from the start. This allows us to take the strengths and weaknesses of each device into account and design something that is not only appropriate for the screen size but also appropriate for the context of use (see Principle 26).

In our studio, by the time we start designing, we have already mapped out all the features and know which devices are most common for our users. This knowledge allows us to make device-specific design decisions based on real requirements and device usage, giving us a higher chance a design that performs well on all of the devices needed.

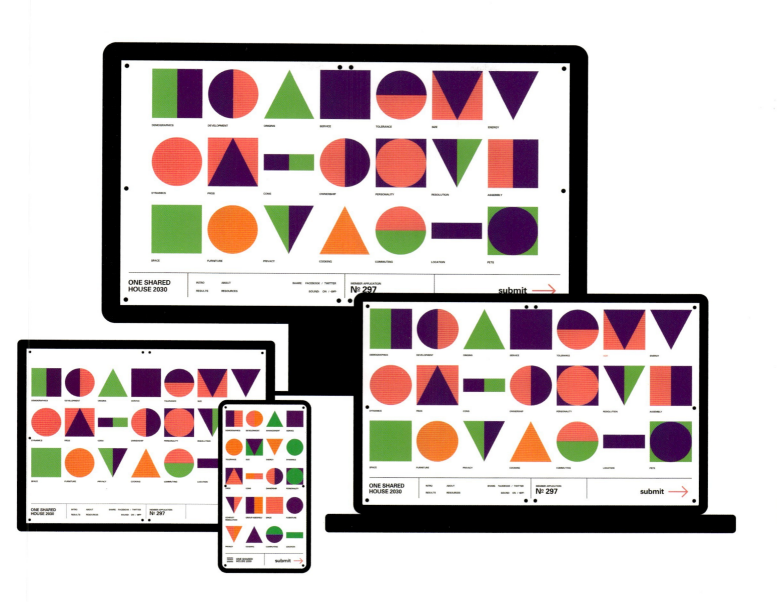

↑
Since we knew people would be accessing One Shared
House 2030 (a project we did in collaboration with SPACE10
and IKEA about the future of communal living) across a
variety of devices, we designed a system that took different
screen sizes and contexts of use into consideration.

Design

85

Systems are great for corporations.

In the early 2000s almost all interesting web experiences were bespoke one-offs made in the now-defunct Flash technology by small design studios. We didn't have to worry about multiple screen sizes because the iPhone had not yet been invented, there were no standards, nobody cared about accessibility (see Principle 18), and all digital interfaces were a pain to update. It was the Wild West: amazing and terrible all at the same time.

Toward the end of the decade, things had started to change. We spent more and more time on mobile screens—which no longer supported Flash—and large corporations were now creating the majority of designs instead of small studios. And since bespoke products take a lot of time to design and are impossible to scale, those large corporations turned to design systems to maintain consistency across their new teams of hundreds of eager designers.

Design systems are about optimizing output and time. They document and modularize common design elements into one source of truth so new designers can easily get up to speed, components can be reused, and users get a consistent experience no matter the device or designer. But since they're very time consuming to create and hard to maintain, it only makes sense to create a design system when you're operating at scale.

That's why design systems are often only created in large corporations. Microsoft introduced now-defunct Metro Design Language in 2010, Google followed with Material Design in 2014, Salesforce and IBM both introduced their design systems in 2015, and AirBnB, Uber, Spotify, and more soon followed suit. What all these large corporations have in common is their massive reach and scale. Without a unified visual language across all devices and screen sizes, it would be impossible to maintain a cohesive look and feel.

From a designer's perspective, design systems turn our creative careers into extremely boring jobs. The restrictions imposed by these systems allow little room for personal interpretation of design elements, making designers feel like production monkeys who merely assemble and no longer design. Even the most senior designers at those types of corporations don't really design. They make decisions and come up with strategies, but they no longer really design.

When bespoke products get replaced by mass-produced design, production speeds up, costs go down, output increases, and brilliant designers get replaced by whoever, all without the loss of any significant amount of quality. Plus, when everything has the same cohesive look and feel, the design becomes easier for people to use. But all these amazing benefits do come at a price. And that price is paid with the designer's freedom, which is why I could never be a designer at any one of those large corporations.

→
When designing for large corporations with established identities (like Spotify), designing something that is consistent across all verticals is more important than the personal expression of the designer.

Spotify Design

Spotify Design

Hey, we're a group of music-loving designers, UX writers, researchers and data scientists making meaningful connections between fans and artists. And we make it all happen by understanding and putting people first.

ALL   DESIGN   INSIGHTS   CASE STUDIES   CULTURE

CASE STUDIES

What's it like to intern at Spotify as a Designer?

05/19/2017 | 12 min read

CASE STUDIES

Redesigning an entire Spotify icon suite.

05/19/2017 | 12 min read

DESIGN

What is good design?

86

Modularity is great for designers.

In our studio, once we have the key pages of the experience designed, we go back and see how we can break the design into smaller chunks so we can reuse those components over and over again across the entire experience. In other words we make the design modular.

When we break the design down into smaller chunks and reuse and combine modules throughout the interface, it allows us—and our developers—to automate the things we don't particularly enjoy working on (like assembling uninteresting but necessary pages like the FAQs or Terms and Conditions) so we can spend more time on the fun parts of the job instead.

To modularize the design, we start by identifying how many unique templates we might need depending on the features listed in the features and functionality matrix. The goal is to keep the number of unique templates to a minimum so we can save time in production and establish a design pattern that users will have to learn only once.

After all the templates are defined, we determine how many unique features we might need. We call these unique features "Lego blocks" (we're '80s kids, after all), and once designed and built, those Lego blocks can be reused across the entire experience or combined to create more complex features. Then it's just a matter of filling the template with all the necessary blocks, adding the copy and images, and boom! We have an actual page of the experience.

This is nothing new or revolutionary. Every design studio has some version of this system. That's because once a design is modular and applied consistently, targeted changes can be made that don't affect the rest of the system. This can be done not just during production, but also years after it has been released, resulting in a more sustainable and maintainable product.

It's important to keep in mind that modularizing design is not something we can easily do retroactively. It takes careful planning and consideration up front, and that planning takes time. But if we do dedicate that time, everybody ends up saving enormous amounts of time later on. And that saved time can then be used to go above and beyond designing and develop the parts of the experience that actually matter (see Principle 44).

→
A small sampling of how often we reused and combined design elements across the website for the M+ museum in Hong Kong. First we designed the key screens, and then we broke the design into smaller components (Lego blocks), which we used to create all other pages.

GOLD SEAT

20 Jan, 2020
28 Feb, 2020

M+ Presents:
The Film Life of Ann Hui

M+與安影人生：安卓的電影人生
Panel Discussion: 11 Jan, 2020
16 screenings

1940—1980

Apply

Screenings

18 Jan	20:00	Get Tickets
19 Jan	14:30	Get Tickets
	20:00	Get Tickets
22 Jan	21:30	Sold Out

Includes post-film wrap-up with director Ann Hui

Includes pre-film discussion with director Ann Hui and the cast

814

Zhang Xiaogang
Bloodline Series- Big Family No.
17-1998

00:14 / 24:34

→ View Object

Audio Transcript

M+ and the West Kowloon Cultural District Authority

M+與西九文化區管理局

Overview

M+ Board

M+ Board Committees

Board of M+ Collections Limited

Getting Here

如何到達M+

Address:
M+, West Kowloon Cultural District,
38 Museum Drive, Kowloon

By Bus

By Taxi / Car

Hourly Parking

By MTR

Accessibility

20 Dec, 2019
12 Apr, 2020

Samson Young:
Songs for Disaster
Relief World Tour

楊嘉輝的賑災專輯 世界巡迴演

Zhang Xiaogang
Bloodline Series- Big Family No.
17-1998

20 Dec, 2019
12 Apr, 2020

M+ Sigg Collection: From Revolution
to Globalisation
Sigg Gallery 3

A Look at Globalisation and Language
in Contemporary Chinese Art.

→ 9 mins / Visual Culture / Article

Our Collections

我們的館藏

We has four permanent collections that are rooted in
Asia but defined, developed, and examined from a
global perspective. Collectively, they form the
backbone of our institution and will continue to evolve
with future generations. Enjoy the richness of our
holdings by exploring the four collections on the right.

Type	+
Language	+
Audience	+
Location	+

24 Jan, 2028

January 2020

Mon	Tue	Wed	Thu	Fri	Sat	Sun
6	7	8	9	10	11	12
13	14	15	16	17	18	19
20	21	22	23	**24**	25	26
27	28	29	30	31

Apply

Akari® Scarf
$1,550.00

Noguchi: A Sculptor's
World
$580.00

Details

詳情

Programme: M+ Presents

Dates: 14 Jan, 2010–28 Feb, 2020

Language: Cantonese (with English Subtitles)

Location: Cinema House 4

Programme Trailer

Tanaami Keiichi: A World of Collages
（Original language）（田名網敬一）

TANAAMI KEIICHI: The reason I liked collages in the
past is that I could gather different materials, place
them down, and then reconstruct them. They formed
a collage that then formed an entire world.

My memories of the past are more important than the
future. The memories of my early childhood are
stronger than more recent memories. Around the
time of the air raids [of World War II], my grandfather
was breeding goldfish as a hobby, right in front of my
house. He used a water tank as big as a tatami mat.
We dug our air raid shelter right in front of the water
tank. When we were in the shelter the water tank was
right in front of our eyes. The American planes
dropped flare bombs. The goldfish tank looked
stunning in that moment as it reflected the light. The
scales on the fish would sparkle. Combined with the
horror of the war, that scene left a strong impression
on me.

These collages were made during the 1960s and early
1970s. My fanatical uncle is closely connected to the
collage materials. He used to collect the magazine
covers and postcards used in these artworks exhibited
here. They were organised tidily based on themes like

M+ Collection

The M+ Collection is an interdisciplinary collection of
visual culture that brings together design and
architecture, moving image, and visual art; works from
Hong Kong, mainland China, elsewhere in Asia, and
beyond.

→ M+ Collection

Zhou Tiehai
周鐵海

14 Jan, 2020
24 Mar, 2020

Location: West Gallery 3

Visit Time: 2 hours is recommended

Queue Time: Average wait times are between
45–55 minutes

M+ Members: Early Access 12 Jan, 2021
Become a Member

Audio Guides: 2024

Get Tickets

Year Donated
2004

Objects
1,510

Period
1979—2012

Collection Objects

Apply

Today	16:00	Design Trust Research Fellowship.
	18:00—20:00	Conversations on Women, Architecture, and the City
	19:45	Shirley Tse: Stakeholders, Hong Kong in Venice
17 Jan	16:00	In the World, Of the World
	18:00—20:00	The Hidden Pulse at Vivid LIVE
	19:45	The Film Life of Ann Hui
18 Jan	16:00—18:30	Conversations on Women, Architecture, and the City
	18:00	Shirley Tse: Stakeholders, Hong Kong in Venice
	19:45	Design Trust Research Fellowship Public Talks
19 Jan	16:00	M+ Live Art: Audience as Performer
	19:45	M+ Matters: Design Trust Research Fellowship Public Talks
20 Jan	12:00	Conversations on Women, Architecture, and the City

M+ Building in Progress
03:40

11 Nov, 2021
6 Oct, 2022

M+ Sigg Collection: From
Revolution to Globalisation
Sigg Galleries

Proceedings: Four Iterations of Hong
Kong in Venice
Researchers & Professionals / Video

M+ Rover Recap 2020

M+ Rover x Lee
Hysan Foundation

Thanks to the generous donation from the Lee Hysan
Family Foundation, the M+ Rover 2020 and 2021
School Outreach Programme brings visual and creative
learning into 50 primary schools, benefiting over
16,000 primary school teachers and students.

"M+ is an exemplar in promoting creative thinking
through the medium of visual culture at schools. The
success of M+ Rover indicates the professionalism,
dynamism and innovative spirit of M+."—Cecilia Ho,
President of Lee Hysan Foundation

→ M+ Rover

Andrew Lee King Fun
North-east elevation (facing Hoi Bun
Road), Pacific Trade Centre, Kwun
Tong, Hong Kong
17 September 1989, revised 1989

LEE HYSAN
FOUNDATION
利希慎基金

C1, D1

P M+ P

The M+ building designed by Herzog
& de Meuron is an iconic presence
overlooking Victoria Harbour.

由Herzog & de Meuron設計的M+大樓是俯瞰維多利亞
海灣的地標。

11	M+ Lounge
5	Research Centre (Accessible via lifts on 5)
3	Roof Garden, Restaurant
2	Galleries
G	Galleries, Grand Stair, Moving Image Centre, Learning Hub, M+ Shop
B1	Restaurant, Cafe, M+ Cinema, Mediatheque, The Other Shop
B2	Found Space, The Studio

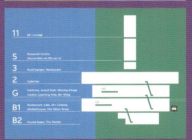

An Introduction to the M+
Collection Archives

This is the first post in a new 'From the Archives' blog
series, which will shine a spotlight on a lesser-known
part of the M+ Collections: the M+ Collection Archives.

→ 3 mins / Design & Architecture / Article

Exploring the Hong Kong Architecture
Archives of Wong & Ouyang

From the Archives: a blog series that shines a
spotlight on the M+ Collection Archives. Below, with
the help of M+ staff members, you can explore...

→ 2 mins / Design & Architecture / Article

Quantity		Ticket Type			Price (HKD)	Subtotal (HKD)
1		Adult			$312	$312
0		Child (ages 6 and below)			$156	$0
0		Child (ages 7–17)			$156	$0
0		Full-time Student			$156	$0
0		Senior (ages 60 and above)			$156	$0
0		Persons with Disabilities			$156	$0
0		Companion for Persons with Disabilities			$156	$0
0		M+ Members / Patron			$276	$0
0		25% Discount Ticket				$0
Total						$312

2012
Gong Jianji
The Second Situation

8802
Unknown (Sanger)
Visit Jiao Bali, Transform Official
Information Bureau of the Motherland

3484
Tobias Tadenari
Diary of a Honoluke
Burger

1212
Belly ren
The Great Pageant
Show

87

Expect the unexpected.

One of the most complex design systems we ever created was part of the *USA Today*'s website redesign in 2012. Not only did we have to create a system that could easily be whitelabeled for all the other newspapers owned by parent company, Gannett, but we also had to make sure that the content management system that powered the entire experience was flexible enough so editors could easily change the priorities of the news articles on the homepage as soon as news would break.

Since every product we build ends up in the hands of the client, we are quite used to building self-publishing tools so clients can make updates to the content on the site themselves. However, in *USA Today*'s case, they needed much more powerful layout options and self-publishing tools than we had ever created before, and it was the first time we gave a client the power to be able to customize the homepage to suit their needs entirely.

We created a variety of different modules (see Principle 86) for very important news, kind-of-important news, and not-so-important news that the editors could pick and choose from to assemble their own version of the homepage throughout the day. We also created separate Lego blocks for developing news (e.g. war coverage), recurring news (e.g., the Olympics or the Oscars), and breaking news. And that's when we got an unusual request.

While we were working through all the different instances and permutations of the breaking news module, Gannett's executive creative director at the time asked us to create what we internally started calling "the 9/11 switch." In one of our many meetings, we discussed how the website's design system would be able to accommodate something like 9/11 happening today.

What we settled on was a disaster layout where the entire homepage would be taken over by one singular article and headline, suppressing all other news stories of the day. This extreme kind of layout would only ever be used in the case of a 9/11-type scenario, and very few people inside *USA Today* would be able to authorize it. In fact, the activation protocols were taken so seriously that we jokingly said it would be easier to fire a nuclear missile than it would be to activate the disaster layout.

The disaster layout thankfully has never needed to be used, but if it had been, we would have been fully prepared. That's ultimately the goal of a good design system: to think ahead and imagine all possible scenarios that could affect the design in the future. If you do, and if you have a solid "if this, then that" logic built into the system, clients are far less likely to accidentally break the design by hacking it to do something it's not designed to do.

→
An example of a normal news day on the *USA Today* website versus what the homepage would look like in the case of a national or international disaster.

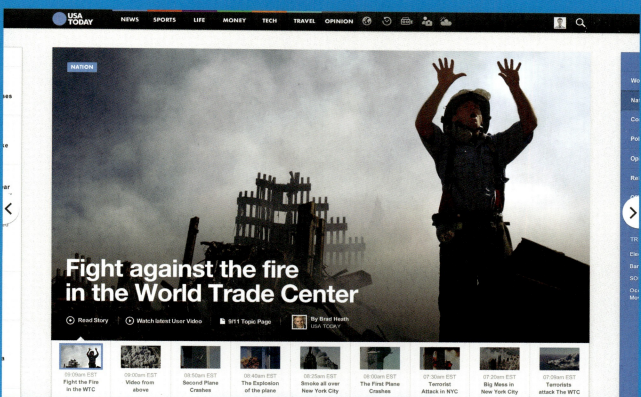

Errors—or any
misunderstand
the result of the
being clear enc
never the fault

nd of
ng—are always
system not
ugh. They're
f the user.

88

Voice assistants suck.

Whenever we talk to Alexa, Siri, or any other voice assistant, we are interacting with artificial intelligence or, more specifically, machine-learning algorithms with natural language processing that utilizes rich data sets to process, understand, and respond to human language. But since communication is such an ingrained part of our biology, we have certain expectations of how that communication is supposed to work.

Voice assistants are supposed to radically improve our lives. They're meant to save us time with our tasks, help people with mobility problems more easily connect to the world at large, and even provide companionship for the elderly. But for all of their progress and the many ways in which they *could* be helpful, voice assistants still fail far too frequently on even the most basic tasks to be dependable. According to research done by Loup Funds, they're wrong anywhere between 10 to 40 percent of the time.

Voice assistants are pretty good at understanding simple verbal prompts, like skipping a song, retrieving the weather, or looking up factoids (unless you have a speech impairment or heavy accent). But they're terrible at understanding the complexity and nuance of human language. They can't fill in any missing details, don't understand things like sarcasm, idioms, context, and metaphors, and can't hypothesize alternatives or future events.

They also don't actually save us any time. Voice assistants requests have to be very specific, and they have to respond in an overly pedantic and long-winded manner to make it clear the request was understood. "Hey Siri, add 'Venus as a Boy' by Björk to my Sunday morning playlist." "Understood, adding 'Venus as a Boy' by Björk to your Sunday morning playlist." In the time spent waiting for Siri to stop talking, I could have added it myself.

And even if they do get much better in the near future, most progress will be made in only the English language. Morphologically rich languages with free word order, like most Slavic languages, for example, make it difficult to train machine-learning models. Plus, it's expensive. Since each language requires its own unique rich data set, it's unlikely that countries with small or poor populations will see investments in voice assistants in the near future.

Having a real, normal, human-like conversation with a computer would be amazing, but only if it is 100 percent accurate, 100 percent of the time. Otherwise it's supremely annoying. And since communication is a two-way street, a failure by one feels like failure by both. So when our communication with a voice assistant inevitably breaks down, not only does it remind us of the types of people and conversations we least enjoy, but also it makes us feel bad about ourselves.

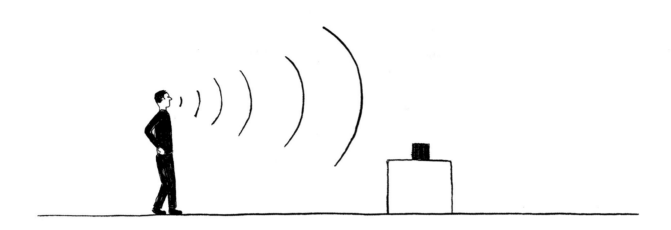

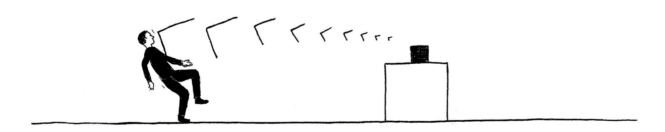

89

Don't ask for unnecessary things.

When I was working at Fantasy Interactive in the 2000s, the founder always used to say that users have three battery cells when it comes to making decisions. They're willing to make one decision and then another, but don't make them choose again after a third option or they're likely to just give up.

We know from usability studies that decision fatigue is a real thing. The more choices we present to a user, the more likely it is that they will abandon whatever it is they're doing (see Principle 24). And that's where defaults come in. When we pre-select things for a user, we minimize the number of decisions they have to make, helping them save time reading or typing, while also making it less likely they'll commit any errors.

There are two types of defaults. The first is educated guesses, which sets the default to the choice the vast majority of users—say, 95 percent—would choose. An example would be when we try to book a flight and the "From" form field is pre-filled with the city we're currently in based on our geo-location data, and the "Depart" form field is already pre-filled with tomorrow's date.

The second type of default is based on information previously provided by the user. Payment details or address and phone numbers can easily be pre-filled if known previously. Or if the system knows that I always send $50 to my cleaner on Mondays—like my bank does—it helps me by pre-filling all that information as well.

When it comes to pre-filling information that might make people uncomfortable—like gender or citizenship—it's best not to make any assumptions. And since people tend to stick to the defaults, it's also extremely important to avoid using deceptive UX patterns that are specifically designed to trick users into something they did not intend to do or benefit only the business (see Principle 5).

Since people tend to think of defaults as a recommendation, they work best when they are personalized, though with the option to change the default easily. After you've gone through the process of thinking through all the different options, go back in and document all possible defaults that will help speed things up. When done right, defaults not only eliminate friction and get people on their way quickly, but they also make it more likely that people will happily return to that product in the future.

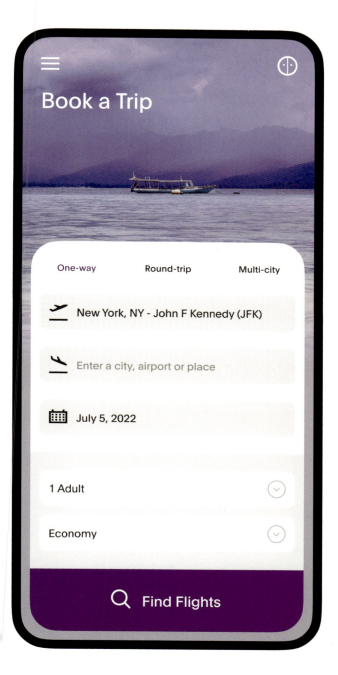

↑
It's helpful to the user when we pre-fill as many form fields as possible based on educated guesses (left). However, it's best not to make any assumptions when it comes to sensitive information, like gender (right).

90

Manage errors effectively.

Recently I tried to log in to my account on the New York State Department website to retrieve a tax document. The first couple of days, the website wasn't working at all—with no explanation as to why or when it would be back online—and when it finally was working, it didn't allow me to log in to my account because, according to the error message, I hadn't changed my username in a while. "Log in first and change your username in your account." What? How am I supposed to do that when it's not letting me into my account in the first place? Absolutely Kafkaesque.

We all know that there is a special place in hell for UX designers who work on any kind of government website in the United States, but that's not what this is about. This is about the responsibility all UX designers have to spot potential errors ahead of time so we can ensure people make as few errors as possible. Errors—or any kind of misunderstanding—are always the result of the system not being clear enough. They're never the fault of the user.

The best kind of errors are the ones that don't occur. Calendars where previous dates cannot be selected, autocomplete prompts that avoid misspellings, or country dropdowns that remove the possibility of someone like me typing out "Holland" when the official name of the country is actually "the Netherlands" are all interaction patterns UX designers use to ensure people can't make an error in the first place.

But we can't remove the possibility of errors entirely. As soon as you are asking the user to type something into a field, there is a chance they'll make a mistake. And when they do, it's important they're able to confidently troubleshoot on their own. This means that the way the system communicates with the user is vital.

Exactly in the area where the error occurred—in a way that draws the user's attention—we have to explain what happened, why it happened, and what the user can do to fix it. Or if the error cannot be resolved by the user (as was the case when the New York State Department website wasn't working at all), we have to explain to the user why the system is down and when it will be back up and running.

Though on the surface it might appear quite simple, error handling actually requires a deep understanding of user needs and the technical capabilities of the system. When error messages are clear, the gap between human and machine communication is bridged, making people not only more comfortable, but also more confident and autonomous in their ability to resolve problems on their own. And trust me, they'd much rather do that than spend hours on hold with customer service or calling some sort of helpline.

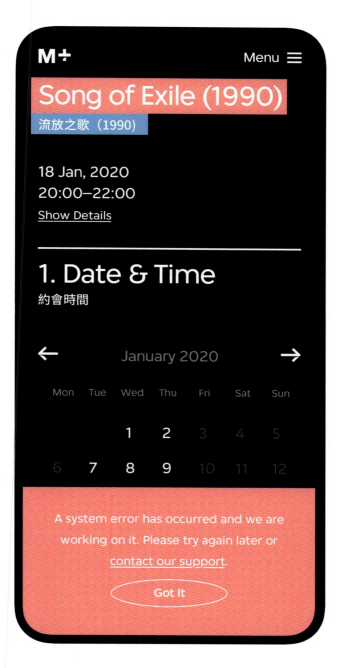

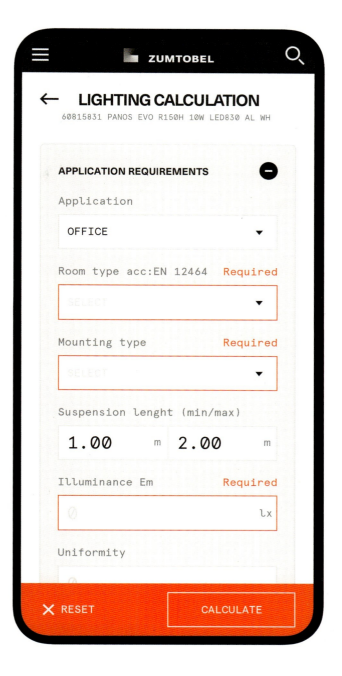

↑
Regardless of what error has occurred, it's important that the system gives appropriate feedback in the appropriate location so users can understand whether the error is beyond their control (left) or something they can resolve on their own (right).

91

Accept many inputs.

Another way to ensure people make as few errors as possible when interacting with an interface is by allowing—and planning for—a variety of different input types from the user. Accepting both uppercase and lowercase on a form or allowing for different file types when adding an attachment or uploading an image are examples of how the design itself has the power to eliminate errors before they even occur (see Principle 90).

This liberal approach to input handling comes from the early '90s and was initially established to allow different computers to use different types of protocols to communicate with each other. Because the internet was a loosely joined distributed system with a variety of implementations that all needed to understand each other, adhering to strict standards would have resulted in many protocol errors and fewer live websites.

Allowing for this type of interoperability was first imagined by one of the early pioneers of the internet, the American computer scientist Jon Postel. When describing an early specification of TCP (one of the main protocols of the internet protocol suite), he famously stated, "Be conservative in what you do, be liberal in what you accept from others." In other words, it was more important for it to *work* than for it to work perfectly.

Although first stated with reference to TCP/IP, it also applied to the parsing of HTML. Since the internet was growing without any kind of centralized control, the idea was that it would be better if browsers would display even poorly or incorrectly written HTML rather than not displaying anything at all.

It also applied to what we accept from users and how we handle what they input on forms. By being flexible about the variety of inputs people might provide—while defining clear boundaries for input—a much larger number of people with various degrees of digital literacy from different devices and browsers are able to interact with the system easily.

When we plan for all the possible idiosyncrasies ahead of time, and the system is more liberal with the types of input it will accept, it allows for an interoperability of many disparate systems which are not—and never will be—under singular control. Though on the surface this might seem insignificant, it's safe to say that without this liberal approach to programming as well as input handling, the internet would never have become as successful as it is today.

→
In the content management system we designed for True, we allowed uploads of a wide variety of image types when creating new pages so there would be a smaller chance for errors.

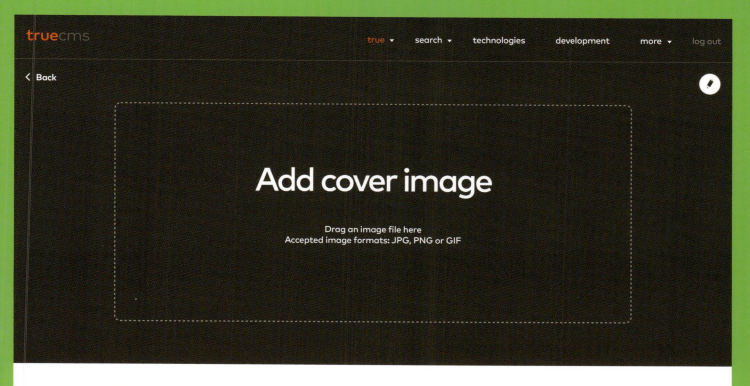

Add cover image

Drag an image file here
Accepted image formats: JPG, PNG or GIF

Title:

Story title

Source tag:

Publication title

Publish date:

Today 04/04/2019

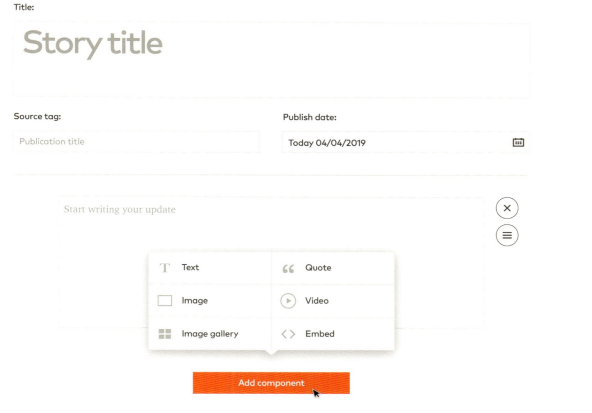

Start writing your update

T	Text	66	Quote
Image		▶	Video
Image gallery		<>	Embed

Add component

92

Confirm user actions.

Whenever I book a class at my gym, I press "Attend," but rather than giving me a confirmation message that I have in fact been successfully added to the class, it just takes me back to the homepage. Huh? Did it work or not? The only way for me to know is to go into my account and double check, adding a totally unnecessary step that could very easily have been avoided by a "You've been registered for the class!" confirmation message right after pressing "Attend."

Besides letting the user know that the system has registered their action, there are instances where it's important to also double check whether or not what the user did is what they intended to do. This deliberate moment of friction might be annoying, but when the user is trying to do something irreversible, or they made a mistake because they try to move through the interface too fast, we need to give people the option to undo or opt out of unwanted decisions (see Principle 14).

However, it's important to keep in mind that asking the user to confirm their choice is needed only for things that are important and irreversible. If they are easily reversible—like retrieving a deleted email from the trash folder—a simple "undo" banner that lingers for a couple of seconds at the top or bottom of the browser is sufficient. If users are bombarded with unnecessary confirmation messages, they might learn to ignore them.

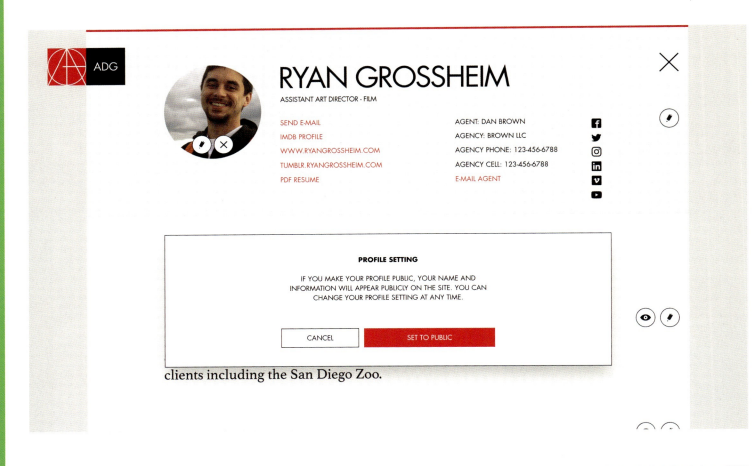

The key thing to remember when designing—and writing—the confirmation message is that it should be as clear and concise as possible, void of any kind of ambiguity. This is one of the places where we need to be extremely explicit and pedantic (but not unnecessarily wordy); if we're not crystal clear, the confirmation message itself could lead to further errors.

When designing and writing a confirmation dialog, it's best to present the user's action back in the form of a question (e.g., "Delete this post?"), explain what the outcome of that action will be ("You will not be able to recover it."), and then once again restate the action in the confirmation button ("Yes, delete post." or "No, cancel.").

As soon as I noticed the lack of a confirmation message, I decided to write to my gym suggesting they add one. I told them I was a UX designer and that they're committing a pretty basic UX no-no, which will lead to many of their customers being unnecessarily confused.

I have yet to receive a reply . . .

↓
Examples of confirmation pop-ups that let the user know when the consequences of their actions are severe (left) or irreversible (right).

93

Broken pages shouldn't feel broken.

If a user mistypes the URL or tries to access a page that requires a log in, they'll end up on a 404 page. If a marketeer accidentally sends out an email campaign with a nonexistent link, people will end up on a 404 page. If the page was deleted or moved but the search engine still has it indexed or the user has it saved as a bookmark, people will end up on a 404 page. A 404 page is the most common error people see on the internet.

One of my favorite internet myths is that the 404 page error was named after Tim Berners-Lee's office while he was working at CERN in the early '80s on what would become the World Wide Web. According to lore, whenever people would go to his office, he frequently couldn't be found, so they assigned his office number as the error code when a user tried to follow a broken or dead link.

Unfortunately for all of us, one of his colleagues at the time, Robert Cailliau, debunked the myth during an interview with *Wired* in 2017. Apparently the 400 range was randomly selected for client errors, and there never even was a room 404 at CERN. How boring. But that doesn't mean the 404 page has to be.

My favorite thing about 404 pages is that they are commonly accepted as the one place where companies are allowed to have a sense of humor. Even the most serious of companies drop their guards on their 404 page. They wink and nod to the user from the other side of the screen, acknowledging their fallibility by breaking the fourth wall. This is why they're one of our favorite pages to work on and why there are entire galleries dedicated to great 404 pages.

It might be tempting to automatically redirect users to the homepage when they encounter a broken link, but that can create even more confusion, especially if they followed that link from their bookmarks or an existing email campaign. So even if we don't make them funny, it's better to at least make the 404 page useful. 404 pages can be used as a navigational aid to help people find whatever it is they're looking for, or if that thing no longer exists, they can help users find something comparable, which is always better than making people feel they've come to a dead end.

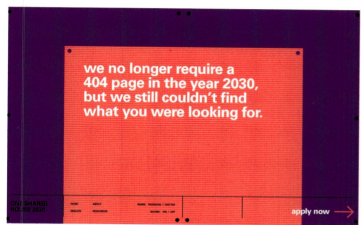

↑
A variety of 404s we have designed over the years. In our studio, 404 pages are never an afterthought. In all examples, the main navigation as well as the search functionality is always accessible by the user, ensuring it's not a dead end.

94

Fill the gap imagination can't bridge.

We don't often make interactive prototypes in our studio. We do a lot of sketches and create a lot of wireframes, but we don't usually make those things clickable. Probably because we never really incorporated them into our process. When we first started in this industry, there weren't any softwares that magically turned static designs into interactive prototypes, so if you wanted one, you had to code it. Interactive prototypes seemed like a luxury back then.

So we learned to work without them. Most importantly, we learned to present to clients and test with users without them. Some people might argue that sketches or wireframes are a prototype, but I don't agree. Wireframes are about how it works, and interactive prototypes are about how it feels. You can test and explain how something works through wireframes and even sketches, but to understand how something feels, you need a more-or-less final UI that people can interact with on their phones or computers.

It's easy to imagine what it might feel like when we press a button to go to another page or how an image carousel might transition, but it's harder to imagine more complicated interactions that rely on new or unusual interaction patterns. When how it feels is not entirely clear, it's very helpful to create an interactive prototype, because they're the only way to fill the gap that our imagination can't bridge.

When we were working with Austrian lighting company Zumtobel, we started work on the homepage after completing all the core pages of the experience. Zumtobel is a very high-end brand and takes great pride in being extremely design focused. They even commission famous artists and designers to do their annual reports (including James Turrell, Anish Kapoor, Stefan Sagmeister, and Per Arnoldi).

Since we knew most people would bypass the homepage anyway (see Principle 70), we had some space to play. We decided to turn some of the annual report covers into full-screen interactive experiences. And to explain what we were imagining, and also understand ourselves how it might feel, we made a lot of different interactive prototypes. How fast should the interface react? What happens on mouse-over? What do we want people to do next?

Did we make interactive prototypes for anything else? No, we did not. We didn't need to, because we used the wireframes to explain how the remaining pages of the experience were going to work. But if we hadn't created the interactive prototypes for the homepage, it would have been impossible to get all of the unusual interactions to feel just right. We wouldn't have been able to imagine it without actually experiencing it first.

Stefan Sagmeister
for Zumtobel Group, 2001-2002

← →

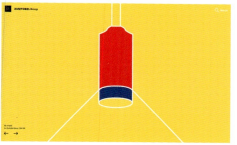

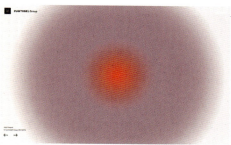

↑
We created a variety of prototypes for Zumtobel to see
how we could make the different covers of the homepage
interactive. This allowed us to make sure the interactions and
animations were appropriate and not annoying.

Validate

95

Metric-based design is silly.

"Yes, it's true that a team at Google couldn't decide between two blues, so they're testing 41 shades between each blue to see which one performs better. I had a recent debate over whether a border should be 3, 4, or 5 pixels wide, and was asked to prove my case. I can't operate in an environment like that. I've grown tired of debating such minuscule design decisions. There are more exciting design problems in this world to tackle."

And that's how Google lost its most prominent designer, Doug Bowman, to Twitter in 2009. It's also the moment Google doubled down on metric-based design and officially sided with engineers over designers. To the wider design community, this signaled that Google believes design is objective and has nothing to do with the intuition or previous experience of the designer (see Principle 52). And since they increased profits by $200 million that year, they seemed to have been right.

But when you look a little closer at those numbers, a different story emerges. According to Statista, Google's ad revenue totaled $22.89 billion in 2009, which means that the increase of $200 million was actually less than 1 percent. And it's not necessarily clear that the new blue links were the reason for that revenue increase. It could have been that more people came online and therefore clicked on more links. Or that the wording of the ads got optimized. Or that they targeted people better. Who knows.

The truth is that Google's ad revenue has been growing steadily each year since they first started running ads in 2000, and it wasn't like there was a massive spike in 2010 the year after they ran this experiment. So they lost their top designer over a 1 percent revenue increase they probably would have gotten anyway.

What's even more ridiculous about this whole experiment is that colors render differently depending on what monitor you are using. And you would think engineers would know that. The blue I see on my monitor is not the same blue you see on your monitor. Even if we have the exact same type of monitor, we probably don't have them calibrated the same. And even if we did, we probably use different brightness settings. My blue link is not your blue link, and it never will be.

Colors aren't even objective to begin with. We see colors differently depending on gender, ethnicity, geography, and even the language we speak. So testing which color blue performs better is silly. And futile. It's also an insult to the design profession. I totally understand why Doug Bowman left Google. Any seasoned and talented designer would die in a place that relegates design decisions to what is a pseudo-science at best (see Principle 53).

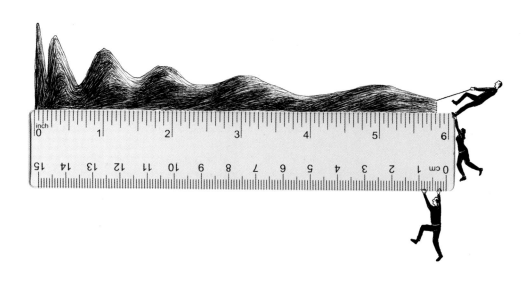

Validate

96

Most issues can be spotted a mile ahead.

Usability tests are designed to collect qualitative and quantitative data to identify potential usability problems before the product gets released. Participants are asked to complete specific tasks—like finding the right support content—while observers watch, listen, and take notes. The goal is to understand how users feel about the design and use those insights to make adjustments to the design prior to launch.

Makes sense, right? I'll let you in on a secret: Over the course of my seventeen-year career, I have only once been surprised by the results of a usability study—only one time. Considering we have completed over 125 separate projects, those are some pretty low odds. Saying this out loud in my field is almost sacrilegious, and I have gotten a lot of heat whenever I would say this at conferences or in interviews. But I'm going to double down.

The only time I was surprised by a usability study was when we were working on the first iPad app for Nickelodeon in 2012. There were two reasons. First we were working with a new medium that we hadn't designed for before (the iPad had just been released), and second we were working with a group of users (children between the ages of six to eleven) we had never designed for before and who have a proven developmental difference from adults when it comes to interacting with computers and interfaces.

I'm not saying extensive usability testing wasn't useful in the 1990s or early 2000s when the mainstream was first coming online and designers were creating some of their first interfaces. But there comes a point where usability testing is a bit silly. Imagine if we would still be usability testing the wheel, knives, or hammers.

If designing for a brand-new medium, device, or target audience, go ahead and perform extensive usability tests. But if we're designing for a commonly used device for the average run-of-the-mill target audience, any UX designer worth their salt should be able to spot usability problems a mile ahead. If they can't, you shouldn't be working with them (see Principle 95).

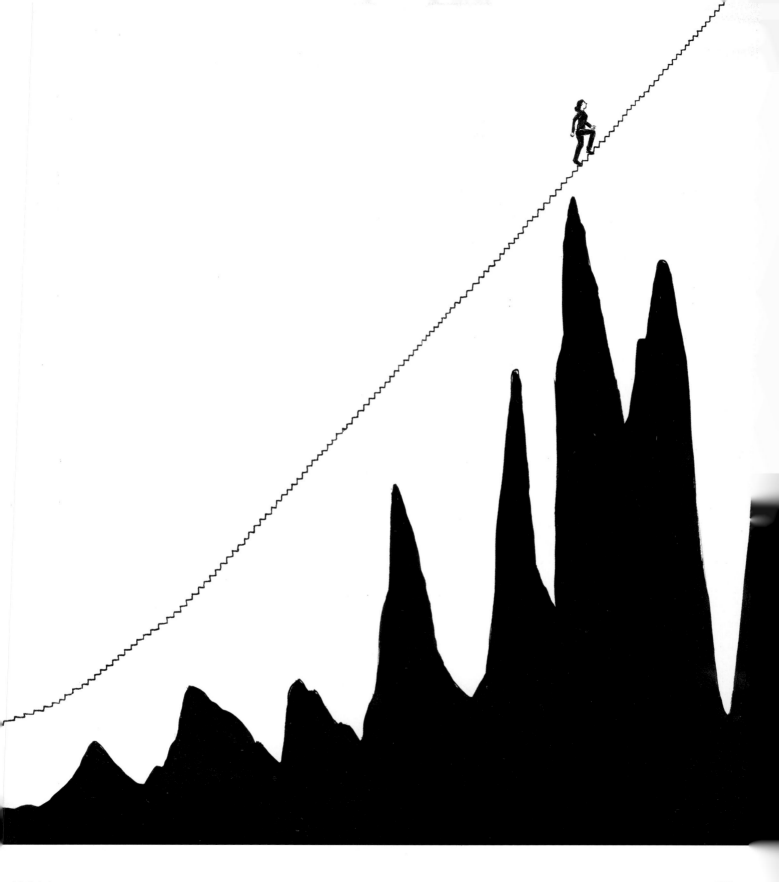

97

Don't grade your own homework.

With my students, I often devise a little experiment to prove a point. I ask them to usability test their own designs, and then I randomly swap their work with another student and ask them to usability test someone else's design as well. And the outcome is always the same. Students always think their own design performs better than it actually does. Why? Because it's extremely difficult to be fully objective when it comes to evaluating your own work.

It might sound like this is a young defensive designer's conundrum, something you grow out of as you become a more experienced designer, but even the most seasoned UX designers have a difficult time avoiding their own confirmation bias. This is why a lot of companies separate the people who do the design from the people who test it. Poorly conducted usability tests can sometimes be worse than no usability tests at all.

So what actually happens, and why are we so bad at evaluating our own work, even if we have the best of intentions? Because we can't help but be emotionally invested. Imagine you've been working on something for weeks or even months. You've done the research, you've gone through the concepting phase, you've sweated about every single little detail, and you've fought many tiny battles along the way to get the design approved. And now comes the moment to test your perfect little baby.

You recruit the right people, set up the right environment, and devise a testing plan that is supposed to unearth insights about the thing you've have obsessed over for weeks or even months. You think you are asking the right questions, have removed all of your biases, and are approaching the whole process with an open mind. You're ready to hear that your baby is ugly.

Except we are not. Whether we like it or not, we are walking into this process with a hidden agenda, and that is to prove that our design works. So rather than being actually open to any feedback or criticism, we have subconsciously created an environment where our assumptions will be confirmed rather than challenged. Because if the design is challenged, we will have to explain ourselves and our design decisions to our client or boss. And who wants to do that?

In my experience, usability testing your own work is a bad idea. Which is why we never do. If a client wants to usability test our designs, I am the first to admit that I am probably not the right person for the job. Just like lawyers shouldn't represent themselves and doctors shouldn't self-diagnose, UX designers really shouldn't be testing their own designs.

98

Get the most
bang for your buck.

A helpful way to understand which parts of the experience should be slated for enhancements and updates first is to look at the analytics to see which pages are currently receiving the highest amount of traffic. It's a bit like redesigning or decorating your apartment or house. Are you going to spend the most amount of effort, time, and money on making sure the living room—where we spend most of our time—looks and feels great or are we going to start with the guest bedroom?

For pretty much everything that is built, only a small amount of pages and functionality will receive the majority of visits and user time. And though we may have a hunch about what is most important, it's helpful to look at the actual time spent on pages to ensure we're not basing our decisions on assumptions. But analytics alone will not tell the whole story. We still have to decide whether to focus our efforts on the top 5, 10, or maybe even 50 percent of user traffic received.

In 1941—some fifty years after Italian economist Vilfredo Pareto first noted that approximately 80 percent of the land in Italy was owned by 20 percent of the population—management consultant Joseph M. Juran developed the Pareto principle, which explained how in quality assurance, 80 percent of a problem is typically caused by 20 percent of the causes. This 80/20 rule is mathematically described by a power law distribution (known as the Pareto distribution) and is a sort of universal law that can be applied to just about anything.

For example, 80 percent of the vegetables in a garden come from 20 percent of the plants, 80 percent of sales come from 20 percent of clients, 80 percent of taxes are paid by 20 percent of people, 80 percent of software bugs come from 20 percent of the features, and most importantly for us UX designers, 80 percent of users only interact with 20 percent of a website's or app's features and pages.

Is it exactly 20 percent? Not necessarily. But thinking of it as 20 percent is a good start. If we focus our attention on the top 20 percent of user traffic and ensure those items are first in line for any kind of enhancement or additions, we can make relatively small improvements that will yield disproportionately powerful results. In other words, focusing on the top 20 percent will ensure that we can make the largest impact for the largest number of users.

That doesn't mean we can just neglect the remaining 80 percent of the experience. It just means that there is less urgency in updating those areas. Eventually we probably do want to do something about that guest bedroom. And repaint the walls. And remove some of the clutter. Even though we might receive guests only a couple of times a year, it's nice to make sure they are as comfortable as possible whenever they do visit.

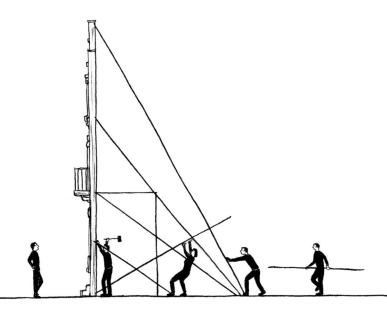

99

Stay involved postlaunch.

This entire book has been written from the perspective of someone who has only ever worked for clients by choice. There have been many instances when I could have worked for SpaceX, Kickstarter, Google, Apple, or a variety of other companies, but working on the same thing day after day, year after year never seemed appealing to me. There's really nothing I envy about working as a product designer, except one thing: being able to stay with a feature or product after it has been launched.

In client projects, there is always this idea of getting everything done and ready for launch. The big push is to get it out into the market, then move on to the next project. Most contracts are set up that way. They start with having conversations about the project and end with launching the project. And that never sat well with me. Mostly because I saw how a product would start to deteriorate when nobody cared for it, or worse, when clients started making random changes that didn't take the user into consideration.

When we started our own studio, we had many discussions about this "love 'em and leave 'em" mentality of client work and decided to make a change. Nowadays, from the very beginning of our conversation with a potential new client, we stress the importance of keeping us involved even after the product is in the market, not on a daily basis, but for at least a handful of hours each month. We tell them we want to coparent the baby.

Staying somewhat involved allows us to see where something might not be working as we expected it to and propose updates or changes that would make certain sections or features better. It also allows us to find out about any operational changes within the company that might affect the product. This has proven to be very important, because we tend to be the only people in the room who understand and defend the user's needs. And since the user's needs are not always fully aligned with the company's needs, the user wouldn't have a voice without us (see Principle 17).

There are no laws that say client projects have to end with launch. If the people who worked on the product keep an eye on how it's doing months or even years after it has gone live, potential problems can be spotted before they even occur. This keeps the product running smoothly, ensuring the user is always part of the equation.

↑
Even though we launched the website for the new M+ museum in Hong Kong in 2021, as of the time of writing, we are still heavily involved and have meetings with their team on a monthly basis. We make sure the website keeps tracking to user goals, new initiatives are incorporated in appropriate ways, and the codebase remains as healthy as possible.

Validate

100

Lower expectations for high satisfaction.

During a project life cycle, many different people across many different disciplines are working on many different parts of the project all at the same time, making it feel a bit like an intricate acrobatic sequence where every move matters. If one person messes up, it has disastrous consequences for everyone else. To minimize the possibility for misalignment, it's important to pause and reflect at key moments.

Let's start with the first moment. Much like preventative medicine, it's helpful to imagine ahead of time what could possibly and potentially go wrong with the project. What are some of the risks involved? Can we imagine where there might be roadblocks along the way? Can we stress test our project plan against extreme delays? Do we have a plan B for all possible scenarios? How quickly are we going to be able to recover or course correct?

The second come-to-Jesus moment needs to occur as soon as something goes out of sync. Even with the tightest project management, it is an absolute guarantee that the team will go slightly out of sync every once in a while. And as soon as it does, the confusion it creates can lead to people getting overworked or working inefficiently, which will generate anger and resentment. So it's best to course correct right away. Because if we don't, the project will literally spiral out of control, dragging everyone else down with it.

The third is after the project has wrapped. At the end of every project, it's important to have a postmortem meeting with both the internal and client team to discuss what went well, what could have gone better, and what we would have done differently knowing what we know today. Yes, it's all water on the bridge now and hindsight is 20/20, but discussing what went wrong previously will help both teams avoid similar mistakes in the future.

Thinking of the worst-case scenario lets the team plan for any potential risks and ensures we don't take it for granted when a project does run smoothly. Because with all of these constantly moving parts, a project that goes according to plan and launches on time is more of a miracle than the norm. So let's lower our expectations and not start the project off assuming it will and safeguard ourselves against the high chance that it won't.

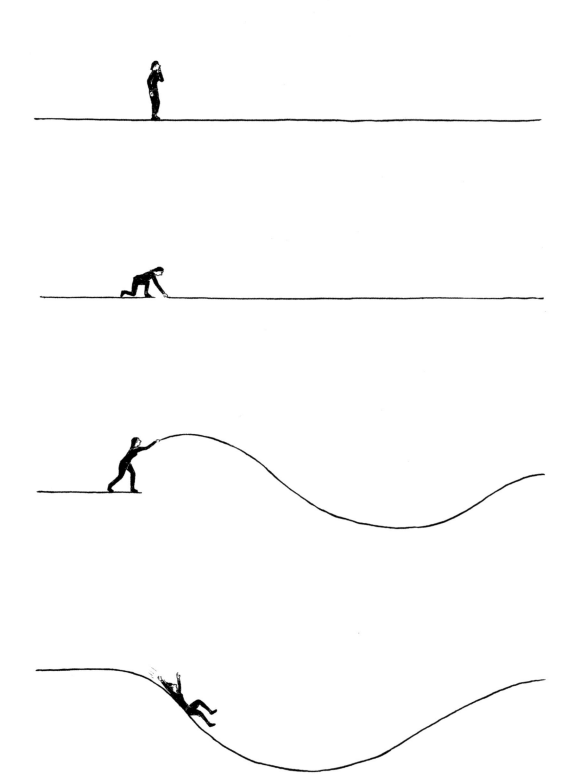

About the Author

Irene Pereyra is the co-founder of the Brooklyn based interaction design studio "Anton & Irene" (antonandirene.com). Since 2007 she has led the strategy and UX initiatives for a large variety of clients and projects, including the Met Museum, the M+ Museum in Hong Kong, the American newspaper *USA Today*, Kickstarter, Balenciaga, Wacom, EA, Adobe, Spotify, Google, Nickelodeon, Karim Rashid, the BBC, Red Bull, the artist Shantell Martin, the Austrian lighting company Zumtobel, as well as a collaboration with SPACE10/IKEA on the future of communal living. The studio also spends three months a year on self-initiated design projects under which the interactive documentary One Shared House, and the NU:RO analog watch.

Her work has been recognized by Cannes, The Webbys, The Emmys, The Red Dot Design Awards, The Adobe Max Awards, The Interaction Design Association, The Society for News Design, The One Show and The European Design Awards. Her personal projects have been shown in Amsterdam, Antwerp, Paris, New York, Copenhagen, London, Cincinnati, Singapore, Barcelona and Tegucigalpa.

Irene has been a guest speaker at over 100 international design conferences, and has lectured at a variety of educational institutions under which SVA in New York, Hyper Island in Stockholm, Elisava in Barcelona, Strelka Institute in Moscow, and the Design Academy in Eindhoven. She is also the chair of the Interaction Design program at Harbour.Space in Barcelona and Bangkok.

Irene holds a Masters of Science in Communications Design from Pratt Institute in New York. Originally from Amsterdam, she now lives in Barcelona with her partner the Argentinian demograher Juan Galeano.

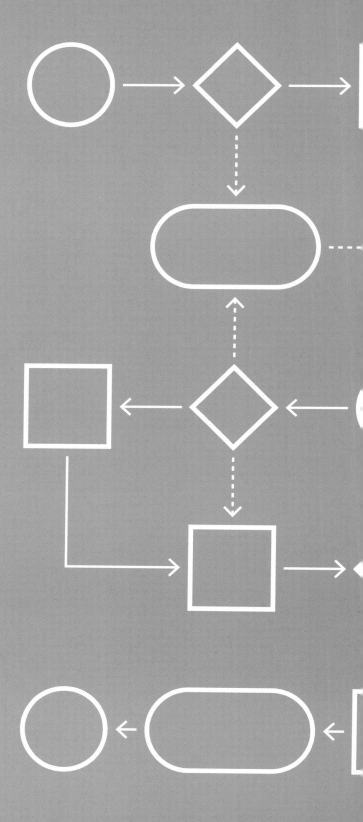

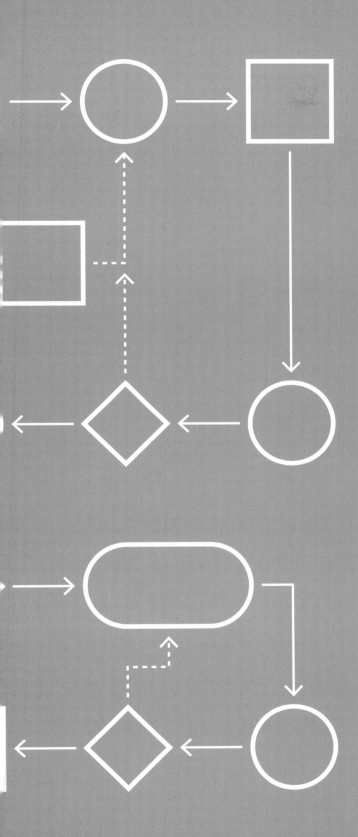

Acknowledgments

This book—along with all the stories in this book—wouldn't have been possible without the constant support of my design partner, and studio cofounder, Anton Repponen. Besides working tirelessly on making sure the design and layouts looked great, he also took on more than his fair share of work during the six month period it took me to write this book. For this I will always be indebted to him.

Two more people are responsible for making this book eminently more readable and understandable—my editor Jonathan Simcosky and the illustrator Vincent Broquaire. Jonathan kept the content focused, highlighted the topics that required more clarification, edited out my cheesy jokes and overuse of metaphors, and gave me the freedom to describe these principles from a more personal perspective. Vincent was the other major contributor to this book. He was responsible for coming up with the incredibly smart and funny illustrations that helped visualize some of the principles, and his clean and beautiful linework added an additional dimension that wouldn't have been possible with words alone.

I would also like to acknowledge my parents Marjan and Rodolfo, and my partner Juan. Without their unshakeable belief in me, I would not have had the guts to put myself out there and write this book.

Lastly this book is dedicated to my students, who for years have helped me clarify and sharpen my understanding of the complex, expansive, and evolving field we have chosen to dedicate ourselves to. If their curiosity, enthusiasm and empathy is an indication of the future of user experience design, it's a bright future indeed.

Index

Quarto.com

© 2023 Quarto Publishing Group USA Inc.
Text, Images © 2023 Anton & Irene, LLC

First published in 2023 by Rockport Publishers, an imprint of The Quarto Group,
100 Cummings Center, Suite 265-D, Beverly, MA 01915, USA.
T (978) 282-9590 F (978) 283-2742

Rockport Publishers titles are also available at discount for retail, wholesale, promotional, and bulk purchase. For details, contact the Special Sales Manager by email at specialsales@quarto.com or by mail at The Quarto Group, Attn: Special Sales Manager, 100 Cummings Center, Suite 265-D, Beverly, MA 01915, USA.

10 9 8 7 6 5

ISBN: 978-0-7603-7804-5

Digital edition published in 2023
eISBN: 978-0-7603-7805-2

Library of Congress Cataloging-in-Publication Data is available.

Design: Anton Repponen and Irene Pereyra
Cover Image: Vincent Broquaire
Page Layout: Sporto
Illustration: Vincent Broquaire

Printed in China